Grow Your Own Pizza

Gardening Plans and Recipes
for KIDS

Constance Hardesty
illustrated by Jeff McClung

Fulcrum Publishing
Golden, Colorado

To my grandfathers, Ronald Hardesty and Sam Martin, who had a special way with tomatoes—and grandchildren. And to AJ Wynkoop—urban farmer, my gardening mentor and #1 father-in-law.

Acknowledgments

Thanks to the many hundreds of kids who have cooked and gardened with me at camps and schools. Your willingness to spit out anything that didn't pass muster certainly helped me hone in on what works!

Special thanks to Rosalind Creasy, Marian Morash, Marjorie Waters, Mollie Katzen, and Jane Brody. Their work continually inspires me to try new things—and provide the solid information I need to succeed. Rosalind Creasy's *Cooking from the Garden* was the main source of information and inspiration for this book.

To the staff at Fulcrum Resources, especially Susan Hill, Patty Maher, Jill Scott, and Marisa Harper. Thanks for your help and enthusiasm in all phases of "growing" this book, and especially in asking Jeff McClung to illustrate it.

And finally, thanks to Graham Kerr and Jerry Baker, my childhood TV tutors, who encouraged me to laugh, muck around, try new things, and say *I can*!

Library of Congress Cataloging-in-Publication Data
Hardesty, Constance.
 Grow your own pizza! : gardening plans and recipes for kids / Constance Hardesty; illustrations by Jeff McClung.
  p. cm.
 Includes bibliographical references
 Summary: Provides plans and instructions for growing twenty-six different gardens, with recipes for using what is grown. Gardens and recipes are divided by difficulty level, from easy to advanced.
  ISBN 1-55591-398-9 (pbk.)
  1. Children's gardens—Juvenile literature. 2. Vegetable gardening—Juvenile literature. 3. Cookery—Juvenile literature. [1. Gardening. 2. Vegetable gardening. 3. Cookery.] I. McClung, Jeff, ill. II. Title.

SB457.H34 2000
635'.083—dc21   99–049793

Printed and Bound in Canada
0 9 8 7 6 5 4 3 2

Fulcrum Publishing
4690 Table Mountain Drive, Suite 100
Golden, Colorado 80403
(800) 992-2908 • (303) 277-1623
www.fulcrum-books.com

Contents

Medium Garden Plots

Advanced Garden Plots

Introduction

You Can Do It!

Imagine if you could grow your own salad ... your own pizza ... your own ice cream! Would it be fun? Would it be good? Could you do it? Of course! *Grow Your Own Pizza* shows you how.

It's Fun

Every garden plan has something to interest or surprise you. The Three Sisters Native American garden uses plants that nourish and protect one another. In the I'm Dreaming of a _____ garden, you grow foods to use in your favorite recipe. There are just so many designs to try out—pizza slices, mazes, forests.

It's Simple

Even if you have never mulched or watered, even if you have never mixed or baked, the easy step-by-step instructions will make it a snap. You don't need an acre of land or any special tools. The gardens will grow in containers, existing flower beds, or small backyard plots. And all you really need is a hose, a shovel, and a rake to make it happen.

It's Healthy

Grow Your Own Pizza shows you how to grow great-tasting food the natural way, without chemicals. Learn to keep your plants healthy and thriving from planting until harvest. Then turn them into healthy, delicious treats!

It's for You

Whatever your age and experience, *Grow Your Own Pizza* has something for everyone. Each garden is different and each recipe is unique, so there is always something new to do and learn. You can use this book for years to come as you move from basic gardens and recipes to more challenging ones.

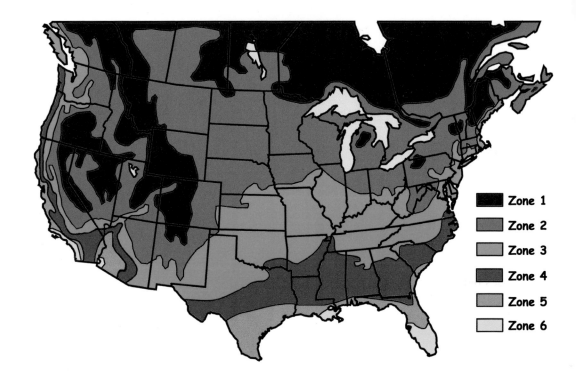

Zone 1
Zone 2
Zone 3
Zone 4
Zone 5
Zone 6

Safe to Plant Dates

Find your location on the zone map above.

Area	Safe to Plant
Zone 1	June 10
Zone 2	May 20
Zone 3	April 20
Zone 4	March 20
Zone 5	February 20
Zone 6	January 30

Tips for the Garden and Kitchen

All gardening and cooking require *active* adult supervision, especially with younger or less experienced children. It's not enough to be in the same room or in the yard with the children. To ensure their safety and their fun, work right alongside them.

Read over all the gardening activities and recipes before starting. Only you can decide which tasks the children are ready to handle and which ones you should do for them. Before allowing children to tackle any gardening or cooking task, be sure they can do it safely.

Garden

- Always garden with an adult.

- Use child-size, child-safe tools.

- Let adults handle sharp tools, including hoes, shears, and shovels.

- Wear gloves, a hat, and sunscreen. Be sure to get the back of your neck!

- Wash your hands after you handle manure, compost, or garden tea.

- Avoid stickers and prickly stems.

- Use natural fertilizers and pest controls. Avoid chemicals that poison children and other living things.

- Stay away from bees, biting bugs, and snakes.

- Keep pets out of the garden and compost.

- Have patience.

- There is no right way to garden. If it works, it's right!

- These are good tasks for children: Planting, weeding, watering, mulching, digging with a child's shovel.

- These are good tasks for adults: Cutting, shoveling, hoeing, pounding stakes.

Kitchen

- All cooking temperatures listed in this book are in degrees Fahrenheit.

- Always cook with an adult.

- Wash your hands before you handle food.

- Before starting, tie back your hair and take off your jewelry. Avoid baggy clothing.

- Thoroughly wash veggies and herbs before cooking or eating them.

- Use only organically grown flowers from a florist for cooking or eating.

- Before you begin cooking, read the entire recipe and gather all necessary tools and ingredients.

- Adjust the position of oven racks before turning on the oven.

- Use thick, dry pot holders to handle hot pans and dishes.

- Keep your hands and face away from steam.

- When cooking on the stove, turn pan handles to the inside of the range, away from other hot burners.

- Avoid touching the edges of cans and can lids. They're sharp!

- When using a vegetable peeler, move the blade away from you.

- When grating food, watch your fingers and knuckles and point the grater away from you.

- Use a cutting board when cutting or chopping ingredients. Always cut away from you.

- Never touch the blade of a knife or vegetable peeler or the sharp edges of a grater.

- If you drop a knife or other utensil, don't try to catch it.

- Let adults wash and dry knives and other sharp tools and put them away.

- Make sure your hands are dry when plugging in electrical appliances. Do not put electrical appliances in water.

- Never put your fingers in an appliance, like a blender or a food processor.

- Turn off the stove and oven when you are finished.

- If grease catches fire, get out of the way and let the adult handle it.

- Use child-safe scissors for snipping herbs or cutting peppers.

- These are good tasks for children: Measuring, mixing, spreading, tossing salads, making sandwiches, mashing with a fork, cutting with child-safe scissors, putting cool foods in the microwave, decorating.

- These are good tasks for adults: Frying, stir-frying, baking, or boiling; handling hot foods, dishes, utensils, or pans; cutting and grating; using food processors or blenders.

Follow the Garden Path to Grow Your Own Feast

In addition to the following tips, refer to The Green Thumb Guide starting on page 107. It includes special tips for making compost and fighting bugs. There are also some secret tips for growing tons of tomatoes!

Dig in the Dirt

Loosen up the soil and mix in lots of nutrients to help plants grow strong.

Get Tough

Take your seedlings outside every day for a week or two before planting time, to help them get used to the sun and wind.

Plants breathe through their leaves and roots. Give your plants plenty of breathing room and keep the soil loose so that air can get down to their roots.

Plant your garden where it will get sun all day.

Plant

The garden plans show you where to put your plants, and the Green Thumb Guide shows how to plant them. The chart on page 6 shows the Safe to Plant date for your region.

Water

Water your garden every day until the seeds sprout.

Thin

Pick the seedlings that crowd their bigger, stronger neighbors.

Water

After the seeds sprout, water the seedlings whenever the soil dries out.

Feed

Give your plants a shovel of manure or a drink of garden tea every two to three weeks. Page 123 tells you how to make garden tea.

Water

Water once a week when there's rain. Water two or three times a week when the weather is hot, dry, or windy.

Mulch

Spread a thick layer of compost, manure, or grass around your plants. This slows down weeds and keeps the soil loose and damp.

Water

Some plants need more water than others; give them an extra drink every week. Each garden plan tells you which plants are extra thirsty.

Weed

Pick every weed as soon as you see it.

Harvest

When your plants are full grown, there will be new things to pick almost every day. Look carefully—lots of veggies hide under leaves.

Feast

Use the recipes in this book to create your own garden feast! You'll find everything you need to know about planting and caring for your garden in the Green Thumb Guide, starting on page 107.

Follow the Garden Path to Your Own Feast

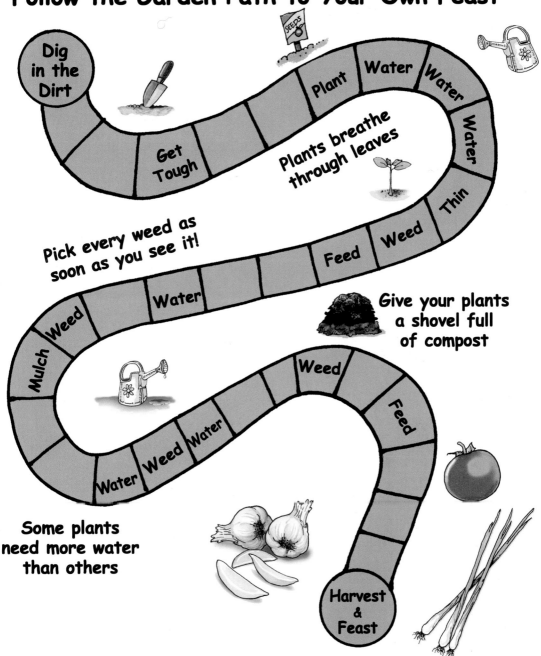

Spring Salad Bowl Garden
Easy

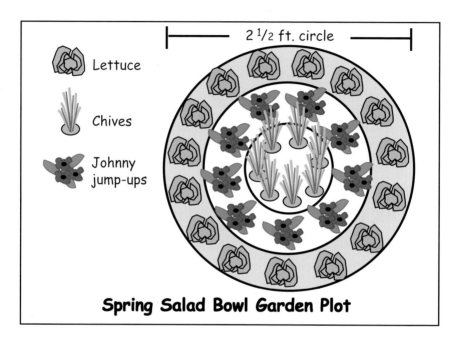

Spring Salad Bowl Garden Plot

- Lettuce
- Chives
- Johnny jump-ups

2 ½ ft. circle

This is the fastest and easiest garden you'll ever grow. The salad fixings look beautiful in the garden and on your plate, too.

You Will Need

3 packets leaf lettuce seeds . . . .

1 clump chives

2 six-packs seedlings for edible . . . . . .
spring flowers

May I Suggest

Salad Bowl, Red Sails, Black-Seeded Simpson

Johnny jump-up (*Viola tricolor*) or edible pansy (*Viola Wittrockiana*)

 Tip You'll find everything you need to know about planting and caring for your garden in the Green Thumb Guide, starting on page 107.

Getting Started

- As soon as the soil is no longer frosty or muddy, plant your garden.

- Plant the lettuce in beds. Use your finger to draw a large square in the dirt. That is your bed.

- Mix all of the lettuce seeds together and sprinkle them over the bed. Press the seeds *lightly* into the soil with your palms.

- Sprinkle the seeds with a *very* thin layer of fine soil—or leave them uncovered. Lettuce seeds need light to sprout.

- Water the seeds using a fine mist from a hose until the soil is damp but not soggy.

Caring for Your Garden

- Lettuce likes lots of water and fertilizer. Give it a drink of garden tea (see page 123) every other week. Be sure to pour the tea on the ground, not on the plant.

- If you see aphids (tiny bugs on the bottom of lettuce leaves), spray them with soapy water. Page 118 tells you how.

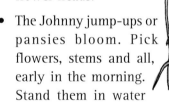

Tip When the weather gets very warm, pull up your lettuce and plant carrots or pretty flowers in its place.

Harvest Your Garden When ...

- The lettuce is 3 or 4 inches tall. Pick all the leaves that are more than 3 inches long.

- The chives are at least 4 inches tall. Use scissors to clip off the leaves and flower heads.

- The Johnny jump-ups or pansies bloom. Pick flowers, stems and all, early in the morning. Stand them in water right away to keep them fresh.

Tip Use the same garden plan for your container garden. Use half barrels as pots!

Leaves
and Flowers Salad
Easy Recipe

The ingredients from your Spring Salad Bowl garden make a lovely salad.

Tools

large bowl for washing lettuce and flowers

paper towels

salad bowl

2 big spoons for tossing the salad

Ingredients

Chive Blossom Dressing

From Your Garden

1 cup small lettuce leaves

6 Johnny jump-up or pansy flowers

Steps

1. Wash and dry the lettuce and flowers. Be *very* gentle.

2. Arrange the lettuce leaves on a plate or in a bowl. Fluff them up so they look nice.

3. Sprinkle 1 tablespoon Chive Blossom Dressing on the lettuce. Toss gently until all the leaves have a little bit of dressing on them.

4. Pick the flowers off the stems and place them on the salad so that it looks pretty.

Chive Blossom Dressing
Easy Recipe

Ingredients

From Your Garden

chive leaves or flowers, or both

From the Market

2 tablespoons apple cider vinegar

1 shake of salt

1 shake (or twist) of pepper

$1/2$ cup light olive oil or vegetable oil

Tools

scissors

measuring cup and spoons

bottle for mixing dressing

small pitcher for serving

Steps

1. Wash the chive leaves and flowers.

2. Use scissors to cut the leaves into tiny pieces. Pick the petals out of the flowers. Throw the centers and stems away. You should have one tablespoon of snipped-up leaves or flowers (or both).

3. Put the chives, salt, pepper, and vinegar in a bottle. Screw the lid on tight. Shake five times.

4. Add the oil to the bottle. Screw the lid on really tight. Shake hard twenty times.

5. Use 1 tablespoon of the dressing to toss the salad. Put the rest in a small pitcher and serve it alongside the salad.

Queen Margherita's Pizza Garden
Easy

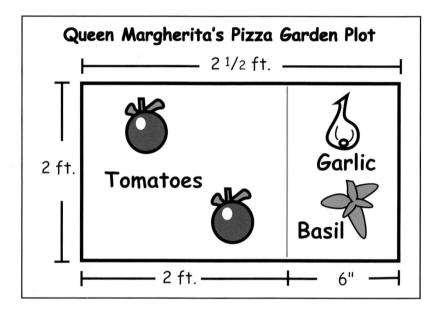

Queen Margherita's Pizza Garden Plot

2 1/2 ft.

2 ft.

Tomatoes

Garlic

Basil

2 ft.

6"

The first pizzas were just chunks of bread topped with whatever was handy. Then, 150 years ago, a famous Italian chef created this special pizza for Italy's pizza-loving Queen Margherita. The pizza shows off the colors of the Italian flag: red, white, and green.

You Will Need

2 cherry tomato seedlings

several cloves of garlic

1 bush basil seedling

May I Suggest

Roma VF (for the best pizza); Red Cherry (for faster harvest)

Spicy Bush or Greek Mini

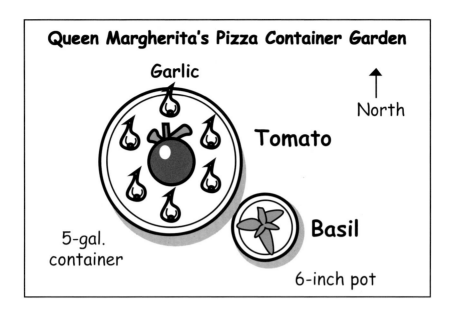

Queen Margherita's Pizza Container Garden

Garlic

North

Tomato

Basil

5-gal. container

6-inch pot

Getting Started

- As soon as the soil is no longer frosty or muddy, plant your garlic.

- Two weeks after your Safe to Plant date, plant the rest of your garden.

- The chart on page 6 shows your Safe to Plant date.

Caring for Your Garden

- This is an easy garden to care for. Just water, feed, mulch, and weed.

- You can grow your tomatoes in cages to help them stand up straight. (Garden centers sell cages.) When the plants are two weeks old, set a cage over each plant and push down gently. As your plants grow, weave the stems in and out of the openings in the cage.

- Pick all the flowers off your basil every day, so the plant will put its energy into leaves, not flowers.

Harvest Your Garden When ...

- The tomatoes are red and soft, but not squishy.

- The basil is at least 4 inches tall and leafy. Take the largest leaves, or pinch off a whole sprig. Leave plenty of green leaves and stems to keep your plants alive!

- The garlic stems fall over and die. Dig the garlic up with your hands so that you don't hurt the bulb.

Tip You will find special tips for growing Tomatoes by the Ton on page 124.

Queen Margherita's Pizza
Easy Recipe

This is one colorful pizza! And you don't need an oven to bake it.

Tools

paper towels

paring knife

scissors

microwave-safe plate

cutting board

mixing spoon

Ingredients

From Your Garden

1 Roma tomato or 4 cherry tomatoes

1 clove of garlic

2 big basil leaves or 4 little ones

From the Market

1 small, ready-made pizza crust, like Boboli™

1 handful grated mozzarella cheese

Steps

1. Wash and dry the tomatoes.

2. If you are using Roma tomatoes, cut out the button on top of the tomato. Then cut the tomato in half. Hold it over a sink or bowl and squeeze gently until the seeds fall out.

3. If you are using cherry tomatoes, cut them in half. If they are large, cut them in fourths.

4. Lay the tomatoes cut side down on a paper towel so that some of the juice will run out.

5. Wash the basil leaves and pat them dry. Use scissors to cut the leaves into little pieces.

6. Place the pizza crust on the microwave-safe plate.

7. Put one clove of garlic on the cutting board and crush it with the back of the spoon. Pick off the papery pieces and set them aside. Rub the spoon around on the garlic, pressing hard. Then rub the back of the spoon all over the pizza crust. This will give you some Italian flavor without overpowering your taste buds.

8. Lay the tomato slices on the pizza crust. Sprinkle the basil over the tomatoes. Sprinkle the mozzarella cheese on top.

9. Cook the pizza in the microwave for 1 minute on medium or until the cheese melts.

Peas 'n' Carrots Garden
Easy

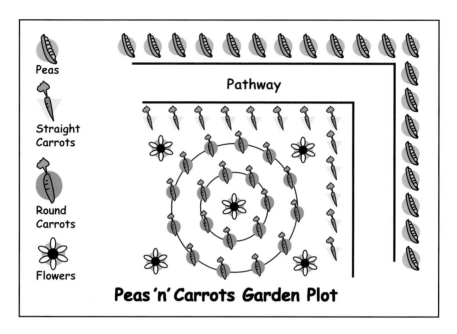

Peas

Straight Carrots

Round Carrots

Flowers

Pathway

Peas 'n' Carrots Garden Plot

Garden peas and carrots are sweet and crisp like fresh, juicy apples. They grow fast, and they don't take much work.

You Will Need

1 package Sugar Snap pea seeds . . . . . .

1 package seeds for straight carrots . . . .

1 package seeds for round carrots . . . . .

May I Suggest

Sugar Ann or Sugar Daddy

Nantes or Half Long

Orbit, Planet, or Thumbelina

WARNING

Do not confuse sugar peas with sweet peas. Sweet peas are poisonous.

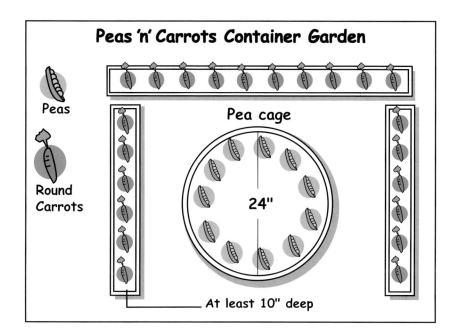

Peas 'n' Carrots Container Garden

Peas

Round Carrots

Pea cage

24"

At least 10" deep

Getting Started

- For the carrots, loosen the soil 6–8 inches deep. This will give your carrots room to grow.

- As soon as the ground is no longer frosty or muddy, plant your peas and carrots. The chart on page 6 shows your Safe to Plant date.

Caring for Your Garden

- Keep your carrot seeds wet, or they won't sprout. Water them *once or twice a day* until they sprout.

- Thin the carrots but don't thin the peas.

- Mulch and weed.

Tip Peas are climbers. Plant them near a sturdy chain-link fence or in cages. Page 23 shows you how.

Harvest Your Garden When ...

- The pea pods are bright green. The bigger the pea, the sweeter it tastes.

- The carrots are at least $1/2$ inch across and start to peek through the dirt. Pull up the ones with the largest tops first. If the first carrot you pull up isn't ready, wait two weeks and try again.

Peas 'n' Carrots 'n' Honey
Easy Recipe

This simple and yummy treat sings with flavor! The recipe makes four servings.

Tools

vegetable brush

paring knife and cutting board

measuring cup and spoons

saucepan

colander

skillet

spoon

pot holder

Ingredients

From Your Garden

2 or 3 straight carrots

1 cup sugar snap peas

From the Market

$1/2$ teaspoon salt

2 tablespoons butter plus 1 tablespoon butter

$1^1/2$ teaspoons honey

Steps

1. String the peas. Scrub the carrots. Trim the top and bottom off each carrot. Then cut the carrots into pieces 1 inch long.

2. Put salt and 8 cups water in a large saucepan. Bring to a boil.

3. Add the carrots. Boil 10 minutes. Drain the carrots in the colander.

4. Melt 2 tablespoons butter in a large skillet over medium heat. Add the peas and stir until all the peas are coated in butter.

5. Cover the pan and cook for 3 minutes, shaking the pan now and then to keep the peas from sticking.

6. Put the carrots on top of the peas. Add 1 tablespoon of butter. Add the honey. Stir until all of the peas and carrots are coated with honey butter. Serve hot.

To plant your peas in a cage, first make a mound that is 1 foot across. Flatten the top of the mound. Plant seeds 2 inches apart all the way around in the top of the mound, near the edge. Buy a large cage from a garden center and set it in the mound after you plant. As the peas grow, weave their stems through the openings in the cage.

Carrots Stuffed
with Spinach Soufflé
Easy Recipe

The orange and green colors in this dish are as brilliant as the garden they come from. The recipe makes twelve servings.

Tools

vegetable brush

paring knife

measuring cup

saucepan

colander

large bowl

paper towels

small melon ball scoop

teaspoon

covered baking dish

pot holder

Ingredients

From Your Garden

12 round carrots, scrubbed and trimmed

From the Market

1 package frozen Stouffer's™ spinach soufflé

Steps

1. Cut a small slice off the bottom of each carrot so that they will stand up straight.

2. Bring 8 cups water to boil in a saucepan.

3. Add the carrots. Boil 8 minutes, or until carrots are barely tender.

4. Fill a bowl with ice water. Drain the carrots in the colander, then dump them in the ice water.

5. Cook the spinach soufflé according to the package directions.

6. Drain the carrots and pat them dry with paper towels.

7. Use a paring knife or melon ball scoop to make a small, shallow hole in the center of each carrot. An adult should do this.

8. Fill the hole in each carrot with spinach soufflé.

9. Put the carrots in the baking dish. Cover and bake at 350 degrees Fahrenheit for 15 minutes. Serve warm.

Sassy Seed Snacks Garden
Easy

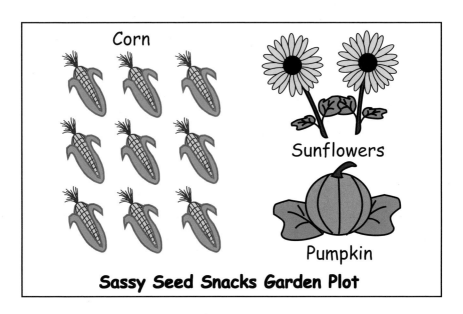

Sassy Seed Snacks Garden Plot

You can grow lots of seeds to snack on—plain roasted, salted, spicy, or sweet. You can bake, boil—or pop!—them.

You Will Need

9 popcorn seeds . . . .

2 sunflower seedlings . . . .

1 pumpkin seedling . . . .

May I Suggest

Strawberry, Pretty Pops, or Miniature Colored

Mammoth for gardens; Sunbird for pots

Triple Treat or Naked Seeded

Getting Started

- After your Safe to Plant date, plant the corn. Soak the seeds in warm water for an hour or so before you plant, so that they will sprout faster.

- Two weeks after your Safe to Plant date, plant the rest of your garden.

- The chart on page 6 shows your Safe to Plant date.

Caring for Your Garden

- Corn needs lots of water and fertilizer. Water at least twice a week, mulch with compost, and give each plant a drink of garden tea every other week.

- When sunflowers are about 1 foot tall, pound a tall (10–12 foot), sturdy stake into the ground next to each one. When the plants are 3 feet tall, use string, a shoelace, or a rag to tie each one loosely to its stake. Do this every 3 feet until the sunflower is as tall as it will get. Then tie one last string under the flower to hold it up.

- When sunflower seeds begin to form, tie a large paper sack over the flower to protect the seeds.

- If your pumpkin plants wilt, you probably have bugs called squash borers. Page 120 shows you how to get rid of them.

Harvest Your Garden When ...

- The corn husks are dry and brown. Twist the ears and snap them off. Shuck the corn and dry it for 4–6 weeks in a warm, dry place.

- The petals fall off the sunflowers. Pick the flower and hang it upside down in a warm, dry place. When the stem is brittle, rub the flower to make the seeds fall out.

- The pumpkins are bright orange. Cut the stem 3 inches above the pumpkin. Be sure to harvest your pumpkins before the first frost!

Popcorn
Easy Recipe

This classic movie treat makes snacks for two.

Tools

measuring spoon

microwave-safe dish with cover

pot holder

Ingredients
From Your Garden

1 ear of popcorn, shucked and dried

From the Market

1 tablespoon vegetable oil

Steps

1. Rub the corn with oil. Be sure to get a little bit of oil on each kernel.

2. Put the corn in the covered dish.

3. Microwave on high about 4 minutes.

 Tip Microwaves cook at different speeds. Watch your popcorn carefully. When 2–3 seconds pass between pops, or if you smell something burning, stop the microwave.

Two Seeds Four Ways
Easy Recipe

There are lots of snacks you can make with sunflower and pumpkin seeds. Here are a few ideas. Experiment with spices to make your own sassy seed snacks!

Tools

knife

paper towels

large bowl

cookie sheet

spoon

pot holder

measuring cup and spoons

saucepan

Ingredients
(for all four recipes)

From Your Garden

1 pumpkin (yields about 6 cups pumpkin seeds)

4 cups sunflower seeds, in their shells, washed

From the Market

2 tablespoons vegetable oil

5 teaspoons salt

6 cups water

1 tablespoon lemon or lime juice

3–4 tablespoons mild chili powder

1 teaspoon black pepper (optional)

1 egg, separated

1 cup sugar

1 tablespoon cinnamon

Roasted Pumpkin Seeds

Steps

1. Cut a pumpkin in half and remove the seeds.

2. Wipe the seeds clean with paper towels. You don't need to wash them.

3. In a bowl, combine 2 cups pumpkin seeds with 2 tablespoons vegetable oil and 2 teaspoons salt.

4. Stir until every seed is coated.

5. Spread the seeds on a cookie sheet. Bake at 250 degrees Fahrenheit for about 1 hour, until the seeds are completely dry. Stir every 15 minutes.

Spicy Seeds

Steps

1. Measure out 2 cups sunflower seeds.

2. Put 2 cups water in a saucepan.

3. Add 1 teaspoon salt, 1 tablespoon lemon or lime juice, and 3–4 tablespoons mild chili powder. If you like your seeds hot and spicy, add 1 teaspoon black pepper.

4. Bring the water to a boil, add the seeds, and boil 5–10 minutes. (The larger the seeds, the longer they need to boil.)

5. Drain the seeds.

6. Spread the seeds on a cookie sheet. Bake at 250 degrees Fahrenheit for $1^1/_2$ hours, until the seeds are completely dried out. Stir every 15 minutes.

Salty Sunflower Seeds

Steps

1. Put 2 teaspoons salt and 4 cups water in a saucepan. Bring to a boil.

2. Add 2 cups clean sunflower seeds. Boil 10 minutes, then drain the seeds.

3. Spread them on a cookie sheet and bake at 250 degrees Fahrenheit until they are completely dry—about $1^1/_2$ to 2 hours. Stir every 15 minutes.

Sweet Seeds

Steps

1. Start with 4 cups pumpkin seeds that are wiped clean but not washed.

2. Beat one egg white.

3. Mix in the pumpkin seeds until they are all coated with egg white.

4. Add 1 cup sugar and 1 tablespoon cinnamon. Stir until all the seeds are coated.

5. Spread on a cookie sheet. Bake at 250 degrees Fahrenheit for 1 to $1^1/_2$ hours, until the seeds are completely dried out. Stir halfway through the baking time.

Be-Kind-to-Animals Garden
Easy

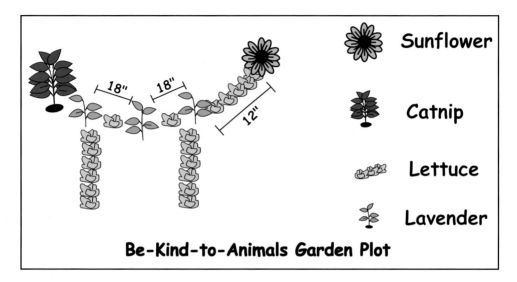

Be-Kind-to-Animals Garden Plot

Sunflower

Catnip

Lettuce

Lavender

Do you have a dog or cat? Bird, lizard, frog, or turtle? Hamster, mouse, or gerbil? Bring them treats from your garden! If you don't have a pet, share your garden with wild birds and squirrels.

You Will Need

2 packages leaf lettuce seeds . . . .

1 catnip seedling

3 lavender seedlings, 1 year old . . . .

1 sunflower seedling . . . .

Tip You'll find everything you need to know about planting and caring for your garden in the Green Thumb Guide, starting on page 107.

May I Suggest

Salad Bowl, Red Sails, or Black-Seeded Simpson

Munstead or Midcote for pots

Mammoth for gardens; Sunbird for pots

Getting Started

• As soon as your soil is no longer frosty or muddy, plant the lettuce.

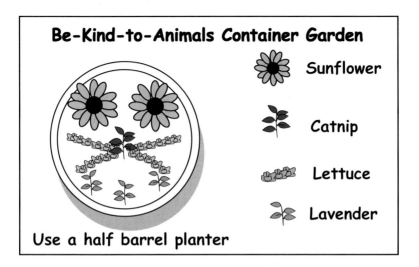

Be-Kind-to-Animals Container Garden

Sunflower

Catnip

Lettuce

Lavender

Use a half barrel planter

- After your Safe to Plant date, plant the rest of your garden. The chart on page 6 shows your Safe to Plant date.

Caring for Your Garden

- Lettuce needs lots of water and fertilizer. Give it a drink of garden tea every other week. Be sure to pour the tea on the ground, not on the plant.

- You don't need to thin leaf lettuce; harvesting will do the job.

- Lavender likes dry soil and no fertilizer.

- When the sunflowers are about 1 foot tall, pound a tall (10–12 foot) sturdy stake into the ground next to each one. When the plants are 3 feet tall, use string, a shoelace, or a rag to tie each one loosely to its stake. Do this every 3 feet until the sunflower is as tall as it will get. Then tie one last string under the flower to hold it up.

- When sunflower seeds begin to form, tie a large paper sack over the flower to protect the seeds.

Harvest Your Garden When ...

- The lettuce is 6 inches tall.

- The lavender flowers open. Pick them early in the day.

- The catnip is 2 feet tall and starts to shrivel. Pick the whole plant and hang it upside down in a warm, dry place. Or strip off the leaves and stems and spread them to dry in a place where your cat can't get them.

- The petals fall off the sunflowers. Pick the flower and hang it upside down in a warm, dry place until the stem is brittle, then rub the flower until the seeds fall out. Or don't pick the flower—let the birds and squirrels find it.

Flea Chaser
Easy Recipe

Try a natural flea collar to keep those nasty pests off your dog.

Tools

an old, clean bandanna

saucepan

pot holder

Ingredients
From Your Garden

2 fistfuls of lavender flowers, fresh or dried

Steps

1. Put the lavender flowers in the pan and cover with water.

2. Simmer 10 minutes.

3. Cool the lavender tea.

4. Soak a bandanna in the lavender tea for 1 hour. Wring it out and let it dry.

5. Tie the bandanna around your dog's neck.

Catnip Toy
Easy Recipe

Nothing makes a cat purr like catnip does. Keep your kitty happy by growing catnip in your garden and making a little toy out of it.

Tools

baking sheet or pan

old, clean bandanna or sock

Ingredients
From Your Garden

several sprigs of catnip

Steps

1. Tear the leaves off the stems.

2. Spread the leaves on a cookie sheet and dry in the oven at 150 degrees Fahrenheit until the leaves break and crumble easily.

3. Stuff the dried leaves in the bandanna or old sock (no holes!) and tie it shut.

Lizard Lettuce

Lizards, turtles, and frogs like a little greenery now and then. Tear lettuce into small bits and drop it in the terrarium or cage.

Sunflower Snackers

Seeds are like candy to gerbils, hamsters, guinea pigs, mice—and birds. Toss a few raw, unshelled seeds in your pet's cage.

Tip Only give your pet 3 or 4 seeds at a time, or it will get fat! You can have a few, too.

Salsa Garden
Easy

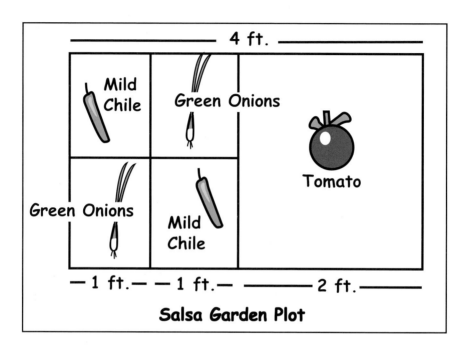

Salsa Garden Plot

Salsa means "sauce" in Spanish. Most salsas you buy taste strong because of the flavorings in them. Salsa made from the garden tastes mild and clean, like fresh air. If you don't like store-bought salsa, try growing some of your own.

You Will Need

1 cherry tomato seedling . . . .

1 oregano seedling . . . .

2 mild green chile seedlings . . . .

1 green onion set

May I Suggest

Red Cherry

Mexican oregano

Anaheim

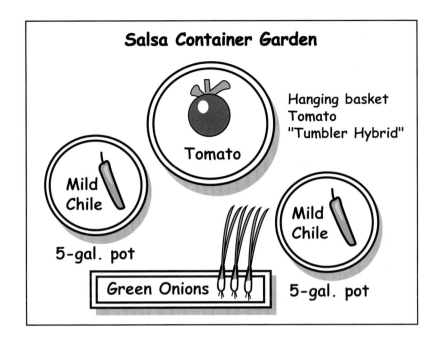

Salsa Container Garden

Hanging basket Tomato "Tumbler Hybrid"

Tomato

Mild Chile

5-gal. pot

Mild Chile

Green Onions

5-gal. pot

Getting Started

As soon as the ground is no longer frosty or muddy, plant your onions. Two weeks after your Safe to Plant date, plant the rest of your garden. The chart on page 6 shows your Safe to Plant date.

Caring for Your Garden

- This is an easy garden to grow. Just water, feed, mulch, and weed.

Tip There are no hot peppers in this garden, because hot peppers cross-pollinate with mild peppers—and make all of them hot! If you want to grow a hot pepper, plant a jalapeño in a pot far away from your garden.

Harvest Your Garden When ...

- The tomatoes are red and soft, but not squishy.

- The chiles are full-size, firm and deep, bright green.

- The green onions are at least 6 inches tall.

- The oregano is at least 4 inches tall and leafy. Take the largest leaves, or a whole sprig. Leave plenty of leaves and stems so that the plant will grow strong!

Mild Garden Salsa
Easy Recipe

Salsa goes with many dishes. This recipe is awesome! It makes 2^1/$_2$ cups.

Tools

paper towels

paring knife and cutting board

bowl

mixing spoon

food processor (optional)

Ingredients

From Your Garden

> 2^1/$_2$ cups tomatoes
>
> 2 green onions
>
> 1 mild green chile
>
> oregano leaves or sprigs

From the Market

> 1 tablespoon mild vinegar (apple cider vinegar or rice wine vinegar)
>
> 1 tablespoon olive oil
>
> 2 shakes of black pepper
>
> Salt to taste

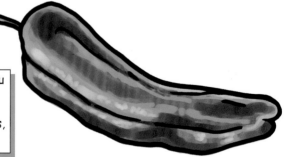

Tip Serve this salsa right away. If you have any left over, freeze it or mix it with a little water and boil it (in a covered pan) for 5 minutes, then store it in the refrigerator.

Dress up your salsa!

Put your salsa in a pretty dish. Make green onion confetti: Trim off the tattered or dirty tops of a green onion. Use scissors to cut the green end into little circles. Stop when you get to the white part.

Sprinkle the confetti around the edge of the bowl. If you have a pepper grinder, make two grindings of black pepper in the center of the salsa. Line a basket with a pretty cloth. Put the dish of salsa in the basket, and surround it with warm tortilla chips. (You can heat the chips in the microwave.)

Steps

1. Wash all the veggies. Dry them with paper towels.

2. Cut the tomatoes into very small pieces.

3. Cut the roots off the green onions. Peel off the outside layer of each onion. Slice the green onions into thin circles. You should have $1/4$ cup.

4. Cut off the top of the green chile. Then slit it open the long way. Take out the seeds and white ribs.

Use child-safe scissors to cut the chile into very small pieces.

5. Tear the oregano leaves off the stems and throw the stems away. Use scissors to snip the oregano leaves into tiny pieces. You should have about 2 teaspoons.

6. Put all the ingredients in a bowl and stir.

7. If you want to use a food processor, cut the tomatoes, onions, and chiles into chunks and put them in the food processor. Add the rest of the ingredients. Blend for 3 seconds. Scrape down the sides of the bowl. Blend for 3 seconds more, or until everything is chopped up and mixed together.

Spot-o'-Tea Garden
Easy

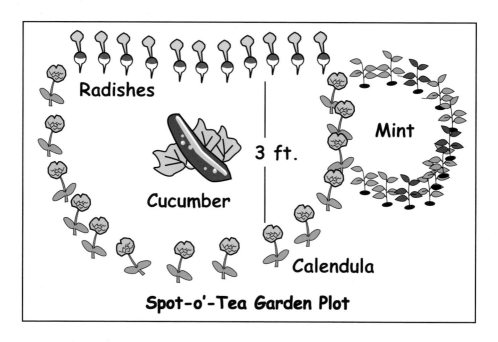

Radishes

Cucumber

3 ft.

Mint

Calendula

Spot-o'-Tea Garden Plot

In England, people eat a small meal called tea in the late afternoon. With goodies from this garden, you can make tasty treats and a soothing drink, too.

You Will Need

1 package radish seeds . . . .

1 cucumber seedling . . . .

1 peppermint seedling

1 six-pack calendula seedlings . . . .

May I Suggest

Easter Egg (for neat colors)

Bush Champion for gardens; Salad Bush Hybrid for pots

Pacific Giant

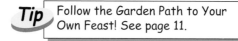

Tip Follow the Garden Path to Your Own Feast! See page 11.

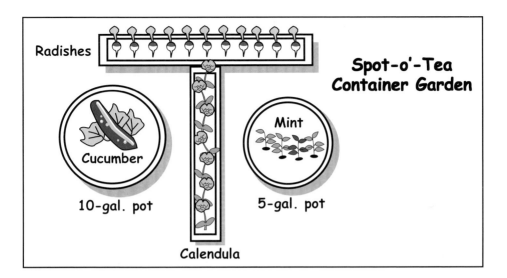

Radishes

Spot-o'-Tea Container Garden

Mint

Cucumber

10-gal. pot

5-gal. pot

Calendula

Getting Started

- As soon as the ground is no longer frosty or muddy, plant your radishes.

- After the Safe to Plant date, plant the mint and calendula. Mint will spread over your whole garden if you plant it in the ground. Keep it in a pot, and put the pot in the garden.

- Two weeks after your Safe to Plant date, plant the cucumbers. The chart on page 6 shows your Safe to Plant date.

Caring for Your Garden

- These plants need lots of water. Water them two or even three times a week when the weather is hot, windy, or dry.

- You can grow cucumbers in cages to make them stand up straight and take less room in the garden. Buy a cage from a garden center and set it over the seedling after you plant it. As the plant grows, weave the stems in and out of the openings in the cage.

- If a cucumber's leaves wilt, the plant probably has a disease. Dig up the whole plant and throw it in the trash.

Harvest Your Garden When ...

- The radishes are the size of a large marble. To find out whether they are ready, just pull one up. Pick the ones with the biggest tops first. Keep harvesting until the radishes are 1 inch across.

- The cucumbers are 3–5 inches long. Cut or twist the cucumber off the stem. Look for new cucumbers every day.

- The calendula flowers open.

- The mint is at least 6 inches tall and leafy. Take the largest leaves, or pinch off a whole sprig. Leave plenty of green leaves and stems to keep your plants alive!

Mint Tea
Easy Recipe

Imagine this: Hot mint tea makes your mouth feel cool. Try it and see! This recipe makes one pot of tea.

Tools

teapot or heat-proof pitcher

measuring cup and spoon

teakettle or saucepan

pot holder

Ingredients
From Your Garden

5 teaspoons

fresh mint

leaves

Steps

1. Wash the mint leaves and put them in a teapot.

2. Boil 2 cups water.

3. Fill the teapot with the boiling water.

4. Let the mixture steep (sit) for 3 minutes. Taste the tea. If it is too weak, add another teaspoon of mint leaves and let steep 2 more minutes.

5. Serve the tea plain or with milk and sugar.

Tip You can also make tea from chamomile, lemon balm, lemongrass, lemon verbena, and pineapple sage. You can try these out in your garden next year.

Tip Would you like a sweet treat at your tea party? Try Berries in a Muffin (page 48). (You can use jam in place of the strawberries.)

Cucumber or
Radish Sandwiches
Easy Recipe

These tea sandwiches are light and pretty. Stick your pinky finger out when you eat them! Makes 24–36 tea sandwiches.

Tools

vegetable brush

paper towels

paring knife

cookie cutter

butter knife

Ingredients

From Your Garden

2 cucumbers or 8 radishes

petals from 1 calendula

From the Market

1 loaf thin-sliced, dense white bread (try English Muffin bread)

butter, mayonnaise, whipped cream cheese, or Rancher Dressing (recipe on page 76)

Steps

1. Wash and dry the cucumbers or radishes. Cut off the ends.

2. Slice the cucumbers or radishes into thin circles. Lay the circles on paper towels.

3. Cut the bread into circles, using a round plastic cookie cutter.

4. Spread the bread circles with butter, mayonnaise, cream cheese, or Rancher Dressing.

5. Put one slice of cucumber or radish on each piece of bread.

6. Pull the petals out of the calendula flowers. Sprinkle a few petals on top of each sandwich.

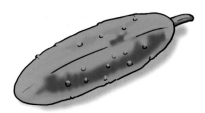

Grow-in-the-Dark Garden
Easy

Most garden plants need many hours of bright sunlight every day to grow strong. But two plants—yeast and sprouts—grow in the dark.

Sprouts in the Closet

You Will Need

$1/4$ cup untreated alfalfa seeds from a health food store

$1/4$ cup untreated radish seeds from a health food store

Getting Started

- Mix the alfalfa and radish seeds together.

- Wet two clean dish towels, then wring them out so that they are damp but not soggy. Lay the towels, one on top of the other, on a cookie sheet.

- Rinse and drain the seeds. Spread them on the wet towels.

- Cover the cookie sheet with plastic wrap and put it in a dark, warm (not hot) place. A high shelf in a closet is a good place.

Caring for Your Garden

- Check on your sprouts every few days. They are very low maintenance, so the only thing you have to do is watch for their harvesting height.

Harvest Your Garden When ...

- The sprouts are about 1 inch long. This usually takes a week. Wrap the sprouts in dry paper towels, then wrap the bundle in plastic wrap. Store in the refrigerator. Eat them within a few days.

WARNING

Don't use treated seeds for planting; they might make you sick. Instead, ask a clerk at a health food store to help you find seeds that are right for making sprouts.

Yeast in a Deep, Dark Bowl
Easy Recipe

Yeast is a live plant. Feed it right and watch it grow.

You Will Need

2 cups lukewarm water

2 packages active dry yeast

2 tablespoons sugar

Getting Started

- Put the yeast, sugar, and water in a large mixing bowl. Stir 10 times.

- Cover the bowl with a plate. If you like, cover the bowl with a towel to make it *really* dark in there.

Caring for Your Garden

- After 10 minutes, look in the bowl. You will see a light brown foam on the water. If you stare at it closely, you will see new yeast plants shooting to the surface in little puffs, like underwater fireworks. That is your yeast growing!

Harvest Your Garden When ...

- You're ready to eat! Leave the yeast in the bowl, but it must be used immediately. Do not let yeast sit if you do not plan to use it right away.

Tip If you put the yeast in water that is too hot, you will kill it. If you put it in water that is too cold, it won't grow. So be sure the water is just right—about 110 degrees Fahrenheit is good.

Best Bread
Easy Recipe

Nothing Smells and tastes as good as fresh baked bread. This easy recipe is fun to make and will make your kitchen smell great. Guaranteed to impress your friends and family! Makes two loaves.

Tools

large mixing bowl

measuring cup and spoons

mixing spoon

cookie sheet

pot holder

Ingredients

From Your Garden

1 batch Yeast in a Deep, Dark Bowl

From the Market

1 tablespoon salt

5-6 cups all-purpose or bread flour

extra flour for kneading

2 tablespoons cornmeal for the pan (optional)

Steps

1. Sift or stir together the salt and flour.

2. Add the flour mixture, one cup at a time, to the Yeast in a Deep, Dark Bowl, stirring as you go. When the dough becomes too stiff to stir with the spoon, use your hands.

3. Sprinkle a little flour on the table where you are going to knead the bread. Dump the dough onto the flour.

4. Let the dough rest while you wash, dry, and butter the bowl.

5. Knead the dough 10–15 minutes. The dough will stick to your hands. Dip them in flour and keep kneading.

Take breaks when your arms get tired. When you have kneaded the dough enough, it will be velvety smooth and elastic. Elastic dough will spring back when you poke it with your finger. Note: If you use an electric mixer with a dough hook, knead on low speed for 4 minutes.

6. Put the dough in the buttered bowl. Cover with a plate. Leave the bowl in a warm place for 1 hour so that the yeast can do its work. When you come back, the dough should be twice as big as it was when you left. It might be even bigger!

7. Gently punch the dough in the middle. It will deflate, like a soft balloon.

8. Divide the dough in half. Gently shape it into two round loaves.

9. If you like, sprinkle the cornmeal onto the cookie sheet. Place the loaves on the cookie sheet.

10. Put the cookie sheet on the middle rack of a cold oven. Set the temperature to 400 degrees Fahrenheit. Bake 35 minutes.

11. Let the bread cool 1 hour before you slice it. If you like, you can cut slices of bread into interesting shapes with cookie cutters.

Sprout Spread Head
Easy Recipe

Who will be first to dig into Sprout Spread's Head?

Tools

spoon

flat surface

Ingredients

From Your Garden

1 handful sprouts

From the Market

8 ounces whipped cream cheese

2 tablespoons raisins

2 tablespoons chopped nuts or roasted sunflower seeds

1 loaf of french bread

Steps

1. Combine cream cheese, raisins, and chopped nuts or sunflower seeds.

2. Form into a ball.

3. Press the sprouts into the cream cheese to make hair.

4. Use raisins or nuts to make eyes and a mouth.

5. Put the Sprout Head in the middle of a large platter. Slice the bread and arrange it nicely around the Sprout Spread Head.

45

Be-Berry-Patient Patch
Medium

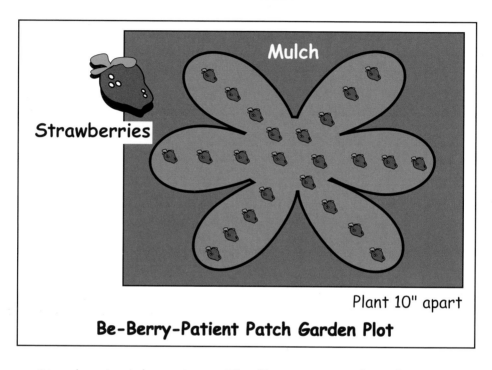

Mulch

Strawberries

Plant 10" apart

Be-Berry-Patient Patch Garden Plot

Strawberries take patience. The first year you plant them, you have to wait until fall for berries. The next year, you will get lots of berries in the spring and again in the fall.

You Will Need
24 everbearing strawberry seedlings

May I Suggest
Ozark Beauty or Tioga; try Fort Laramie in cold areas

Getting Started
- Find a spot where your strawberries can grow for two or three years.

- Two or three weeks before your Safe to Plant date, check the soil. If it is not soggy or frosty, plant your berry patch. The chart on page 6 shows your Safe to Plant date. Plant the strawberries in mounds (page 109 shows you how).

Caring for Your Garden

- Keep your berry patch tidy. Pick the baby plants that branch off the large plants. Clean up dead leaves and fallen berries.

- Mulch with compost. To make a clean, dry bed for the ripe berries to rest on, spread a layer of sawdust, straw, grass clippings, or leaves over the compost.

- Here's the challenge: You *must* cut all the flowers off your plants until July. If you don't, your plants will not grow strong. In the fall, you will get more flowers and then berries.

- If birds or critters start to eat your berries, cover the whole garden with bird netting. (You can buy the netting at a garden center.)

- When the weather gets cold, cover the whole berry patch with a thick blanket of straw, leaves, or grass clippings. This will help your strawberries survive the

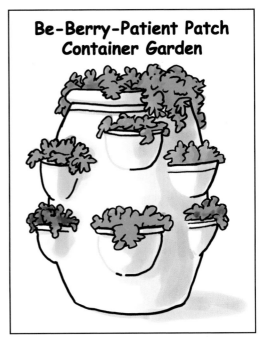

Be-Berry-Patient Patch Container Garden

If you are growing strawberries in pots, store them in their pots in a garage or other cold, sheltered place for the winter. Take them outside again in early spring.

Be sure that the place where the roots meet the leaves is exactly at ground level when you plant. Otherwise, your plants will rot.

winter. Early next spring, carefully rake off the mulch.

Harvest Your Garden When ...

- The strawberries are red and soft, but not squishy. Pinch the stem with your fingernails 1 inch above the strawberry. Pick ripe strawberries every day, or the birds will get them.

- The first year, harvest strawberries in the fall. Next year, you can harvest in spring *and* fall.

Berries in a Muffin
Medium Recipe

There's a sweet surprise hidden inside these muffins! Makes twelve muffins.

Ingredients
From Your Garden

24 strawberries the size of your thumbnail

From the Market

baking spray

1 package muffin mix

OR

1 egg

3/4 cup milk

1/2 cup vegetable oil

1 cup flour

1/3 cup sugar

3 teaspoons baking powder

1/2 teaspoon salt

cinnamon sugar (2 tablespoons sugar mixed with 1 teaspoon cinnamon)

1 cup oatmeal (not microwave oatmeal)

Tools

2 muffin tins

sharp knife

measuring cup and spoons

2 mixing bowls

fork

mixing spoon

teaspoon

pot holder

 Tip You can use mini-muffin tins if you have them. Use just one strawberry in each muffin cup. Makes 2 dozen mini-muffins.

Steps

1. Preheat the oven to 400 degrees Fahrenheit.

2. Spray muffin tins with baking spray.

3. Wash and dry strawberries. Remove the stems, hulls, and leaves.

4. Make muffin mix according to the package directions. Or, put the flour, oatmeal, sugar, baking powder, and salt in a bowl and mix it up.

5. In another mixing bowl, beat the egg with a fork. Stir in the milk and oil.

6. Add the flour mixture all at once and stir gently until the flour disappears. The batter should still be lumpy.

7. Fill each muffin cup about one-third full. Drop in two strawberries. Cover them with muffin batter. Each muffin cup should be about three-fourths full.

8. Sprinkle with cinnamon sugar.

9. Bake 15–20 minutes.

Strawberry Punch
Easy Recipe

Wash down your muffins with a bit of punch! Makes four glasses.

Tools

paring knife

bowl

fork

pitcher

mixing spoon

Ingredients
From Your Garden

2 cups strawberries

From the Market

4 cups orange juice or lemonade

Steps
1. Wash the strawberries. Remove the stems, hulls, and leaves.

2. Cut the berries into small pieces.

3. Put them in a bowl and mash with a fork until there are *no* lumps.

4. Put the strawberries in a pitcher. Add the orange juice or lemonade. Stir.

 Tip You can make strawberry ice cubes for your drink: Put one cleaned, trimmed strawberry in each compartment of an ice cube tray, add water, and freeze.

Corn Crop Circles Garden
Medium

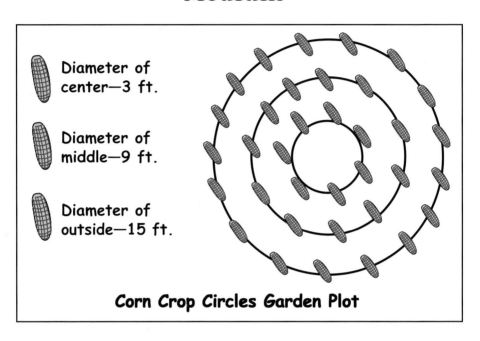

Diameter of center—3 ft.

Diameter of middle—9 ft.

Diameter of outside—15 ft.

Corn Crop Circles Garden Plot

Corn is one of the most popular vegetables in the United States. It's not the easiest plant to grow and it takes lots of space, but it tastes wonderful. This compact design is inspired by the mysterious circles that keep cropping up in England.

You Will Need
2 packages corn seeds · · · · · · · · · · · · · · ·

May I Suggest
Gold Rush Hybrid for early harvest

Kandy Corn or Honey and Cream for later harvests

 Tip Soak your corn seeds in warm water for a few hours before you plant to make them sprout faster.

Getting Started

- After your Safe to Plant date, plant the corn. The chart on page 6 shows your Safe to Plant date.

Caring for Your Garden

- Corn needs lots of water and fertilizer. Water your garden at least twice a week, mulch it with compost, and give it a big drink of garden tea every other week.

Tip You'll find everything you need to know about planting and caring for your garden in the Green Thumb Guide, starting on page 107.

Harvest Your Garden When ...

- The corn is juicy and the silks are brown and dry. Peel back a little of the husk and poke one of the kernels with your fingernail. If a milky liquid comes out, the corn is ready. If the liquid is clear and watery, the corn is not ripe yet. (Close the husks and wait a few weeks, then try again.) If the corn is tough and dry, it is old.

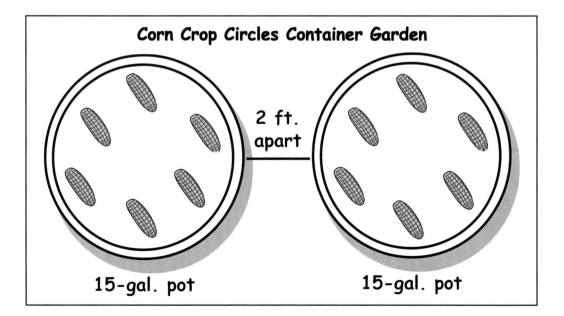

Corn Crop Circles Container Garden

2 ft. apart

15-gal. pot   15-gal. pot

Cobs and Cobs and Cobs of Corn
Easy Recipe

Any way you prepare it, corn tastes delicious. If you want your corn and want it now, here are a few easy recipes to create with this favorite vegetable.

Tools

vegetable brush

waxed paper

microwave-safe dish

tablespoon

stock pot

steamer rack

patio grill

charcoal

tongs

Ingredients

From Your Garden

4 ears of corn for each recipe

Microwave Corn on the Cob
Steps

1. Shuck the corn and remove the silks.

2. Wrap each ear in waxed paper and put them on a plate, or place all 4 ears in a microwave-safe dish with 2–3 tablespoons of water.

3. Cover and microwave on full power 6–8 minutes.

Steamed Corn
Steps

1. Shuck the corn and remove the silks.

2. Put the steamer rack in the stock pot. Add 1 inch water and cover the pot. Bring water to a boil.

3. Place the corn on the steamer rack. Cover and steam about 6 minutes.

Tip Let an adult handle the hot, cooked corn.

Roasted Corn on the Cob

Steps

1. Peel back the green leaves, but leave them attached.

2. Remove the silks.

Tip To remove the silks, rub gently with a vegetable brush.

3. Rinse the corn, then fold the leaves back up over it. If they won't stay shut, tie them with cooking string.

4. Fill a sink with water and soak the corn for 10 minutes.

5. Place the corn on a grill over hot coals or in an oven at 450 degrees Fahrenheit for 10 to 15 minutes.

Campfire Corn on the Cob

Steps

1. Build up a fire, then let it die to coals.

2. Follow the directions for Roasted Corn on the Cob, but lay the corn right on the coals.

3. Roast 10 minutes. Turn the ears often (with tongs) so that the corn doesn't burn.

4. When the husks start to turn black, the corn is done.

The Best Boiled Corn

Steps

Corn starts to lose its sweetness the second it comes off the stalk. That's why old pros wait until the last minute to pick their corn. Here's an old-timer's recipe:

1. Fill a stock pot two-thirds full of water and put it on to boil.

2. When the water boils, put on your running shoes and tie them tight. Race out to the garden, grab two ears of corn, shuck them on the fly, and throw them in the pot. Don't lose a second. If you so much as stumble, throw out the corn and start over!

Tip Use potholders and tongs to handle hot corn.

Your Personal Pizza Garden
Medium

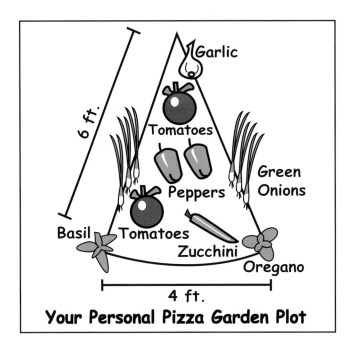

Your Personal Pizza Garden Plot

You can't grow *everything* you need to make a pizza, but you can grow lots of goodies to pile on top! Start by listing the veggies you like on your pizza. Then grow your own Personal Pizza Garden.

You Will Need

1 oregano seedling

1 bush basil seedling

2 tomato seedlings

1 green onion set

2 bell pepper seedlings

1 package zucchini seeds

several cloves of garlic

May I Suggest

Mexican oregano can take the heat

Spicy Bush, or Purple Globe

Roma VF for the best pizza; Pixie or Tom Thumb for pots

California Wonder or Earlired

Aristocrat

Getting Started

- As soon as the soil is no longer frosty or muddy, plant your onions and garlic.

- After the Safe to Plant date, plant the rest of your garden. Some plants, like corn or sunflowers, can be planted right away. Tender plants, like tomatoes, peppers, basil, and zucchini, need more heat. Wait a few weeks after your Safe to Plant date before putting them in the ground.

- If you are unsure about when to plant something, check the seed package or plant tag. Or ask a clerk at the garden center when you buy the plants.

- The chart on page 6 shows your Safe to Plant date.

> **Tip** It's OK if your garden doesn't match the drawing. This is *your* pizza garden—plant what you like!

Caring for Your Garden

- Some plants, like peppers and zucchini, love water. Keep the soil around them damp all the time. Other plants, like onions, garlic, tomatoes, and herbs, need less water.

- If your zucchini plants wilt, you may have borers. Page 120 tells you what to do.

- Pick all the flowers off your basil every day so that the plant will put its energy into leaves, not flowers.

- Grow your tomatoes in cages to help them stand up. (Garden centers sell cages.) When the plants are two weeks old, set a cage over each plant and push down gently. As your plants grow, weave the stems in and out of the openings in the cage.

Harvest Your Garden When ...

- The green onions are at least 6 inches tall.

- The garlic stems fall over and die. Dig the garlic up with your hands so that you don't hurt the bulb.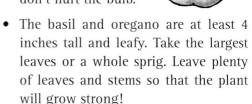

- The basil and oregano are at least 4 inches tall and leafy. Take the largest leaves or a whole sprig. Leave plenty of leaves and stems so that the plant will grow strong!

- The tomatoes are red and soft, but not squishy.

- The peppers are brightly colored (green or red) and the size of a small apple.

- The zucchini are about 5 inches long.

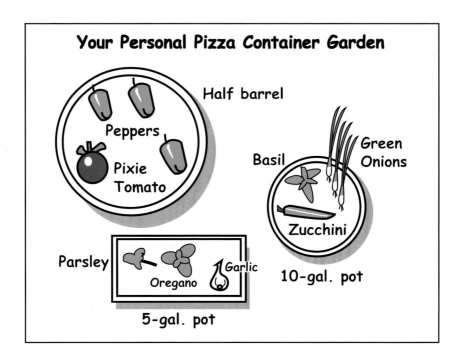

Your Personal Pizza Container Garden

Half barrel

Peppers

Pixie Tomato

Basil

Green Onions

Zucchini

10-gal. pot

Parsley

Oregano

Garlic

5-gal. pot

One Pizza Twelve Ways
Medium Recipe

Pizza is one of those foods that always taste great. This recipe makes twelve pieces, so invite some friends to a pizza party from your own personal pizza garden!

Tools

vegetable brush

paper towels

paring knife and cutting board

several bowls (cereal bowls are good)

scissors

cookie sheet

mixing spoon

can opener

table knife

pot holder

Ingredients

From Your Garden

3 small tomatoes or 1 big one

1 clove of garlic

12 basil leaves

(Whatever else you grew: 4 oregano leaves, 1 sprig parsley, 1 sweet red pepper, 2 small onions, and as much as you like of other favorites.)

From the Market

1 pizza crust (packaged in a roll in the refrigerated section of the market)

8-ounce can tomato sauce

2 cups mozzarella cheese

Tip How much will you need? Start with one of each vegetable you like. If that's not enough, run to the garden to get more. If you have more than you need, make a salad!

Steps

1. Wash and dry all the veggies and herbs.

2. Cut out the button on the top of each tomato. Cut the tomatoes in half from top to bottom, then hold them, cut side down, over the sink and squeeze gently until most of the seeds fall out. Chop the tomatoes into small pieces and put them in a bowl.

3. Using scissors, cut the herbs into small pieces. Toss the snipped herbs with your fingers to mix them.

4. Chop the veggies into small pieces. Put each veggie in a different bowl.

5. Spread the pizza crust in a pan according to the instructions on the package.

6. Put one clove of garlic on the cutting board and crush it with the back

of the spoon. Pick off the papery pieces and set them aside.

7. Pick up the smashed pieces of garlic and rub them over the whole pizza crust.

8. Spread a thin layer of tomato sauce all over the pizza crust.

9. Using the table knife, draw lines in the tomato sauce to mark off 12 equal-size pieces.

10. Put different pizza toppings in each square. Sprinkle the mozzarella cheese on top.

11. Bake the pizza at 400 degrees Fahrenheit for 25 minutes.

Superfoods Garden
Medium

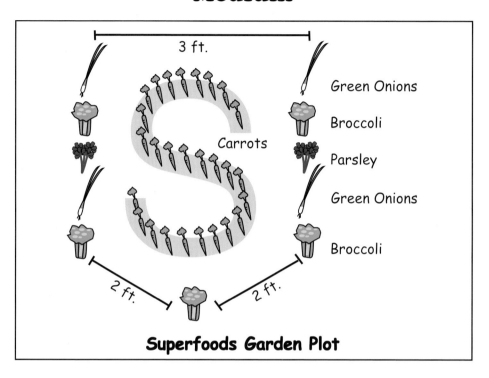

Superfoods Garden Plot

3 ft.

Green Onions

Broccoli

Carrots

Parsley

Green Onions

Broccoli

2 ft.   2 ft.

The veggies in this garden are so good for you that scientists call them Superfoods. They're super for dips and sauces, too! Carrots, onions, and parsley are easy to grow. Broccoli takes a little more work.

You Will Need

1 four-pack of broccoli seedlings

1 green onion set

2 packages carrot seeds

2 curly parsley seedlings

May I Suggest

Premium Crop for gardens, Green Comet for pots

Nantes or Royal Chantenay

Extra Curled Dwarf

Getting Started

- As soon as the ground is no longer frosty or muddy, plant your garden.

- For the carrots, loosen the soil 6–8 inches deep. This will give your carrots room to grow.

Caring for Your Garden

- Carrots and broccoli like lots of water. Keep the soil damp all the time.

- Put mats around your broccoli seedlings when you plant them to protect them from worms. Also look for holes in the leaves—that means you have tiny green cabbage worms. You can pick them off, or let them be. If you don't have too many worms, you will still get a harvest before the worms kill the plant.

- Page 118 tells you how to make mats.

Harvest Your Garden When …

- The broccoli heads are full and tight, about 8 inches across. Harvest them right away, before the flowers begin to open. Use a knife to cut the stalk a few inches below the head. During the next few weeks, look for smaller heads on the same plant.

- The carrots are at least $\frac{1}{2}$ inch across and start to peek through the dirt. Pull up the ones with the largest tops first. If the first carrot you pull up isn't ready, wait two weeks and try again.

- The parsley is at least 4 inches tall and about 8 inches across. Break the stems off at the ground. Leave plenty of leaves and stems for the plant to grow strong!

- The green onions are at least 6 inches tall.

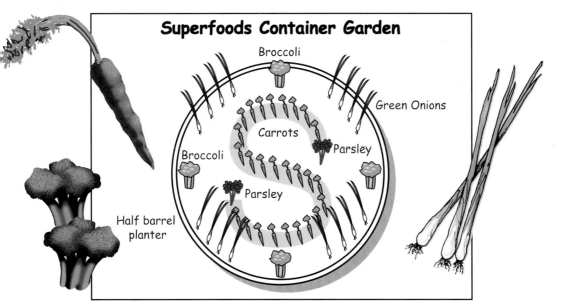

Superfoods Container Garden

Broccoli

Green Onions

Carrots

Broccoli

Parsley

Parsley

Half barrel planter

Broccoli Trees
Under a Green Cheese Moon
Medium Recipe

How could you not try this yummy salad? Makes one big salad.

Tools

vegetable brush

paring knife and cutting board

large bowl

measuring spoon

scissors

small mixing bowl

mixing spoon

colander

saucepan

pot holder

paper towels

salad plate

Ingredients
From Your Garden

1 head broccoli

1 green onion, green part only

1 small sprig parsley

2 carrots

From the Market

2 tablespoons salt

1 small tub soft (whipped) cream cheese

2–3 tablespoons milk

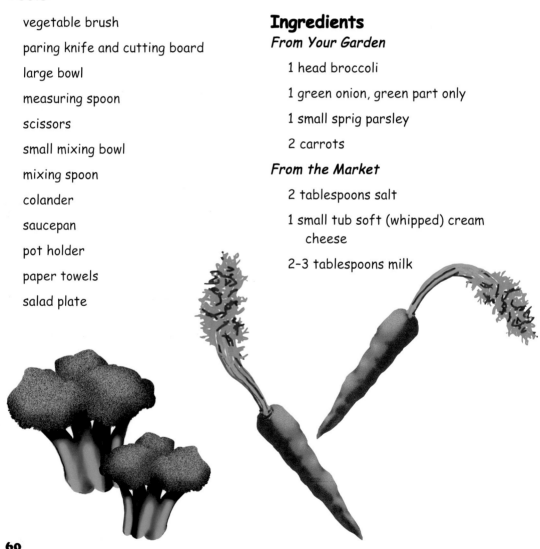

Steps

1. Wash the broccoli. Cut off the stalk just under the head. Break the head into clumps (called florets).

2. Fill a large bowl with water. Stir in 2 tablespoons salt. Dump in the florets and let them soak.

3. While the broccoli is soaking, make the Green Cheese dressing. First, use scissors to snip the parsley and green onion into tiny pieces. In the small mixing bowl, mash together the cream cheese, 1 tablespoon green onion, and 3 teaspoons parsley. If the dressing seems too thick, stir in some milk, a little bit at a time, until it is right.

4. Drain and rinse the broccoli. Look for tiny green worms in the florets and pick them off. Look hard—they are good at hiding!

5. Fill the saucepan with water and bring to a boil. Add the broccoli florets and boil 5 minutes.

6. Drain the broccoli, then drop it into a bowl half full of ice water. Let the broccoli cool 15 minutes. Then drain and dry the florets with paper towels.

7. Scrub the carrots and trim off the leaves and root end. Cut the carrots into sticks.

8. To make the salad, arrange the carrots, broccoli, and dressing on a plate like this:

9. If you have leftover parsley and green onion, sprinkle it around the bottom of your "tree."

Cake and Ice Cream Garden
Medium

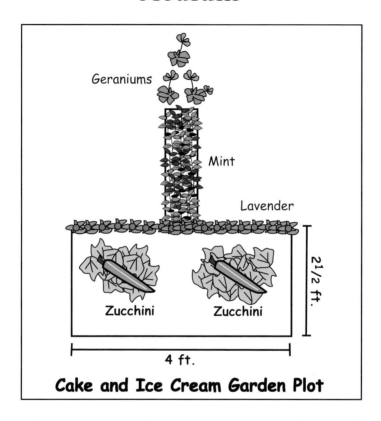

Geraniums

Mint

Lavender

2½ ft.

Zucchini   Zucchini

4 ft.

Cake and Ice Cream Garden Plot

Do you know anyone with a summertime birthday? Throw a surprise party starring cake and ice cream you made from the ground up!

You Will Need

1 package zucchini seeds . . . .

1 peppermint seedling

3 rose geranium seedlings

3 lavender seedlings, 1 year old . . . .

May I Suggest

Aristocrat is green and holds its fruit off the ground; Gold Rush is golden, which makes a pretty cake

Lavandula augustifolia; try Munstead or Midcote in pots

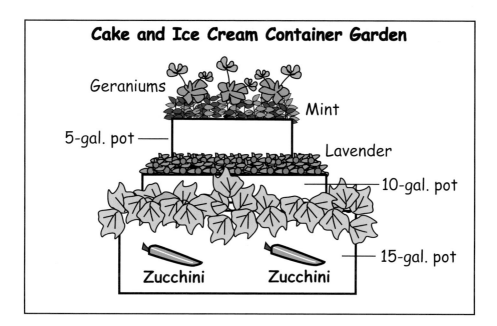

Cake and Ice Cream Container Garden

Geraniums · Mint · 5-gal. pot · Lavender · 10-gal. pot · 15-gal. pot · Zucchini · Zucchini

Getting Started

- Two weeks after your Safe to Plant date, plant your garden. The chart on page 6 shows your Safe to Plant date.

- Plant your mint in a pot and put the pot in the garden. Mint will spread over your whole garden if you plant it in the ground.

Caring for Your Garden

- Mint and zucchini like lots of water. Always keep the soil around them damp. Lavender and geraniums don't need as much water; give them a drink every other time you water the rest of the garden.

- If your squash plants wilt, you may have borers. Page 120 shows you what to do.

Harvest Your Garden When …

- The zucchini are about 5 inches long.

- The mint is at least 4 inches tall and leafy. Take the largest leaves, or pinch off a whole sprig. Leave plenty of green leaves and stems to keep your plants alive!

- The lavender flowers are showing color, but are not fully opened. Cut whole stalks early in the day.

- The rose geranium flowers first bloom. Pick them early in the morning, when their flavor is strong.

Tip You'll find everything you need to know about planting and caring for your garden in the Green Thumb Guide, starting on page 107.

Chocolate Zucchini Cake
Medium Recipe

Have your cake and veggies too! Makes cake for twelve to sixteen people.

Tools

knife and cutting board

grater

colander

9 x 13 pan

large microwave-safe bowl

mixing spoon

measuring spoons and cups

flour sifter or medium-size bowl and fork

pot holder

Ingredients

From Your Garden

3 cups zucchini, grated

From the Market

baking spray

3 squares baker's (unsweetened) chocolate

1 $1/2$ cups vegetable oil

3 cups sugar

4 eggs, beaten

3 cups flour

1 teaspoon salt

1 $1/2$ teaspoons baking powder

1 $1/2$ teaspoons baking soda

1 cup chopped walnuts

Steps

1. Measure out 3 cups of the zucchini.

2. Working over the sink, pick up a big handful of zucchini and squeeze it like you would a snowball. Water will run out. Squeeze hard until the water stops dripping.

3. Put the squeeze-dried zucchini in a colander. Repeat until all the zucchini has been squeeze-dried.

4. Preheat the oven to 350 degrees Fahrenheit. Coat the pan with baking spray.

5. Put the chocolate in a microwave-safe bowl. Microwave it on medium-low for 1 minute, then take it out and stir it.

6. Continue to microwave the chocolate on medium low, stopping and stirring every 30 seconds, until the chocolate is melted.

7. Stir the oil into the chocolate.

8. Stir in the sugar and eggs.

9. Sift together the flour, salt, baking powder, and baking soda.

10. Dump all at once into the chocolate mixture and stir until smooth. (If you don't have a sifter, put the ingredients into a bowl and stir them with a fork.)

11. Add the zucchini and nuts. Mix well.

12. Pour the batter into the pan and bake 1 hour, until a toothpick inserted in the center of the cake comes out clean.

13. Cool in the pan 20 minutes, then turn out onto a cake rack.

14. After the cake cools, sprinkle it with powdered sugar or flower petals.

Peppermint Ice Cream
Medium Recipe

Peppermint ice cream—refreshing, creamy, *and* delicious! Makes about 1 quart (by volume) of ice cream.

Tools

measuring cup and spoons

heavy saucepan

pot holder

mixing spoon

ice cream maker

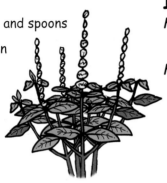

Ingredients

From Your Garden

8 peppermint leaves, washed and dried

From the Market

1 cup whole milk

1 cup whipping cream, cold

$1/2$ cup sugar

2 egg yolks, beaten

5 peppermint candies, crushed

Steps

1. Combine peppermint leaves, milk, whipping cream, and sugar in the saucepan.

2. Heat over very low heat, stirring constantly, until small bubbles begin to form around the edge of the pan.

3. Cool 10 minutes. Pick out the peppermint leaves or strain the milk through a fine sieve. Cool 10 minutes more.

4. Add 1 tablespoon of the cream mixture to the egg yolks and mix well. Repeat three times. This warms the egg yolks so they won't be shocked and curdle in step 5.

5. Pour the egg mixture into the cream mixture in the saucepan. Cook over medium heat, stirring constantly, until small bubbles again form around the edge of the pan and the mixture coats the spoon.

6. Cool again to room temperature. Add the peppermint candies.

7. Freeze in an ice cream maker according to the manufacturer's instructions.

Tip If you don't have an ice cream maker, just follow this recipe through step 6. After the milk mixture cools, pour it into a 9- by 13-inch baking pan and put it in the freezer. After 10 minutes, take it out of the freezer and chop and stir the ice cream up with a spoon. Do this every 10 minutes until the ice cream is frozen.

Rose-Scented Geranium Cake
with Lavender Ice Cream
Medium Recipe

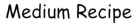

This lovely, unique treat smells too good to eat. It's perfect for a warm summer evening.

Tools

two 8-inch round cake pans

spatula

measuring cup and spoons

heavy saucepan

pot holder

mixing spoon

ice cream maker

Ingredients
From Your Garden

8 rose-scented geranium petals, washed

1 tablespoon lavender petals

From the Market

1 white cake mix

1 cup whole milk

1 cup whipping cream, cold

$^1/_2$ cup sugar

2 egg yolks, beaten

whipped cream

Steps

1. Butter and flour two 8-inch round cake pans, then line the bottom with clean rose-scented geranium petals.

2. Make a white cake mix according to the directions on the package.

3. After you bake the cake, turn it out onto a rack and pick off the flowers.

4. Frost the cake with whipped cream and decorate with rose geranium petals.

5. To make the ice cream, follow the instructions for peppermint ice cream, but use lavender petals in place of the peppermint leaves. (Leave out the peppermint candies.)

67

Pickles 'n' Peppers Garden
Medium

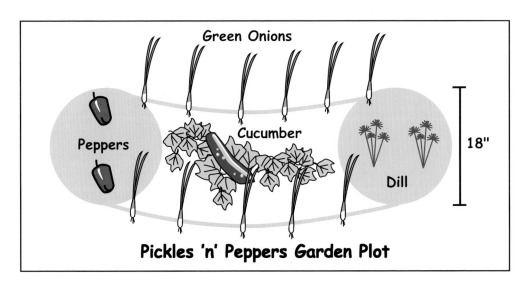

Pickles 'n' Peppers Garden Plot

Labels in image: Green Onions, Peppers, Cucumber, Dill, 18"

Pickles are easy and fun, and you can make them out of anything you like—zucchini, cauliflower, green beans, peas, watermelon rind—even pigs' feet! We'll stick to the old standby—cucumbers.

You Will Need

1 pickling cucumber seedling . . . .
1 green onion set
2 red cherry pepper seedlings . . . .
2 dill seedlings . . . .

May I Suggest

Liberty, Burpee Pickler, or West Indian Gherkin

Sweet Cherry

Dill Bouquet for pots

Tip Pickling cucumbers are different from regular cucumbers.

Getting Started

- As soon as the ground is no longer frosty or muddy, plant your onions.

- Two weeks after the Safe to Plant date, plant the rest of your garden. The chart on page 6 shows your Safe to Plant date.

Caring for Your Garden

- These plants love water! Always keep the soil damp.

- You can grow cucumbers in cages to make them stand up straight. Buy a cage from a garden center and set it over the seedling after you plant it. As the plant grows, weave the stems in and out of the openings in the cage.

- If a cucumber's leaves wilt, the plant probably has a disease. Dig up the whole plant and throw it in the trash.

- It is OK for dill to turn yellow after it has been growing awhile.

Harvest Your Garden When ...

- The cucumbers are about 4 inches long. Look for new cucumbers every day— they grow fast. To pick, cut or twist the cucumber off the stem.

- The cherry peppers are bright red and the size of a big marble.

- The dill forms big flower heads with buds. Pick whole sprigs (stems with leaves and flower heads) before the buds open.

- The onions are at least 6 inches tall. Pick every second onion, to give those left behind room to grow.

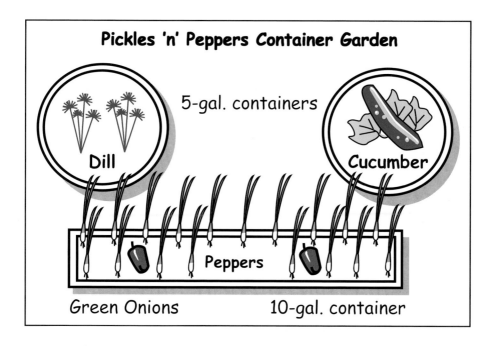

Pickles 'n' Peppers Container Garden

5-gal. containers

Dill

Cucumber

Peppers

Green Onions   10-gal. container

Dill Pickles 'n' Peppers
Medium Recipe

Spicy and tangy all in one! Makes 3 pints.

Tools

- sharp knife
- cutting board
- measuring cup and spoons
- colander
- paper towels
- large glass bowl
- spoon
- 3 pint-size freezer containers or storage bags

Ingredients

From Your Garden

- 6 slim cucumbers, 3–4 inches long
- 3 red cherry peppers, with $1/4$ inch of stem on
- 3 green onions
- 6–8 sprigs fresh dill (sprigs should be about 6 inches long with lots of leaves and flower heads in bud, not in bloom)

From the Market

- 2 tablespoons pickling or kosher salt (*not* table salt!)
- 1 cup sugar
- 1 cup white vinegar

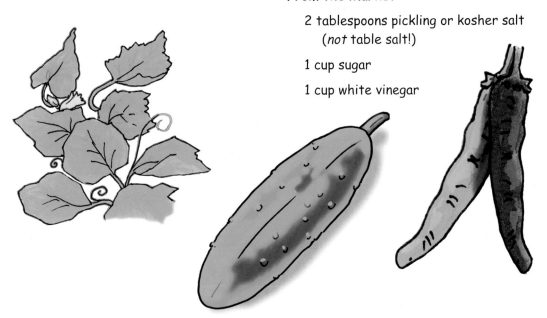

Steps

1. Wash the vegetables and dill very well.

2. Trim the ends off the cucumbers, then cut the cucumbers into thin slices.

3. Trim the green onions and cut them into pieces 3 inches long.

4. Put the cucumbers in the colander and sprinkle with 2 table-spoons pickling salt. Stir. Let stand 2 hours. The salt draws some of the water out of the cucumbers, so that the pickles won't be mushy.

5. Rinse the cucumbers under cold running water for 1 full minute. Stir the cucumbers as you rinse them to be sure all the salt washes off. Pat them dry with paper towels.

6. In the glass bowl, combine the dill, sugar, vinegar, and 1 tablespoon pickling salt. Stir until the sugar is dissolved.

7. Add the vegetables. Mix well.

8. Pack the vegetables into the freezer bags or containers. Be sure to divide the brine (liquid) evenly among all the containers.

9. Freeze.

10. Defrost in the refrigerator at least 8 hours before eating.

Rainbow Garden
Medium

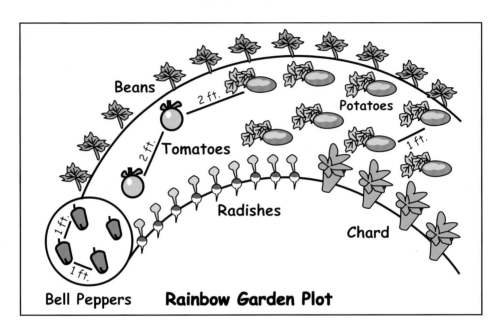

Beans

2 ft.

Potatoes

2 ft. Tomatoes

1 ft.

1 ft.

Radishes

Chard

1 ft.

Bell Peppers **Rainbow Garden Plot**

Surprise your family and friends with purple beans, blue potatoes, bright yellow tomatoes, orange peppers, ruby chard, and pastel radishes. Your garden will look lovely, and after the harvest you will be eating rainbows.

You Will Need

2 packages radishes . . . . Easter Egg

2 packages chard seeds . . . . Ruby Swiss

8 seed potatoes . . . . All Blue

2 packages colorful bean seeds . . . . Royalty or Royal Burgundy

4 orange bell pepper seedlings . . . . Tequila Sunrise or Gypsy

2 yellow tomato seedlings . . . . Yellow Pear for gardens; Golden Pygmy for pots

May I Suggest

Getting Started

- As soon as the ground is no longer frosty or muddy, plant the radishes, chard, and potatoes.

- After your Safe to Plant date, plant your beans.

Tip Soak your bean seeds in warm water for a few hours before you plant them to make them sprout faster.

- Two weeks after the Safe to Plant date, plant your tomatoes and peppers.

- The chart on page 6 shows your Safe to Plant date.

Tip Before you plant the potatoes, dig around in the ground to loosen it 18 inches deep. This will give your potatoes room to grow. To plant potatoes, make sure each seed potato has at least two eyes. Plant the potatoes 4 inches deep and 18 inches apart with the eyes facing up.

Caring for Your Garden

- Chard is slow to sprout. Don't give up: Keep watering every day until it does.

- Radishes and peppers love water. Keep the soil around them damp all the time.

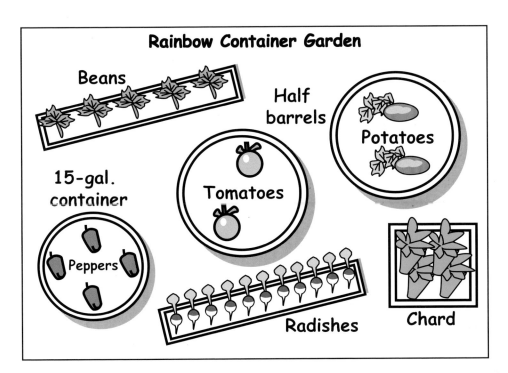

Rainbow Container Garden

Beans

Half barrels

Potatoes

15-gal. container

Tomatoes

Peppers

Radishes

Chard

- When potatoes are about 6 inches tall, pile 1 inch of dirt right up against the stems. Do this every other week until harvest.

- You can grow beans and tomatoes in cages to make them stand up straight. (Garden centers sell cages.) When the plants are two weeks old, set a cage over each plant and push down gently. As your plants grow, weave the stems in and out of the openings in the cage.

- If the leaves of your beans get very holey, you have Mexican bean beetles. Harvest all the beans you can, then dig up the plant and throw it away.

WARNING

Fruit will form on your potato plants. Don't eat it—it is poisonous to people and animals! Potatoes are tubers—they grow underground.

Harvest Your Garden When ...

- The radishes are the size of a marble. Pick the ones with the biggest tops first.

- The chard plants have 6–8 big leaves. Pick a few leaves from each plant at a time.

Tip After you harvest the chard and radishes, you can plant flowers in their place.

- The beans are 3–4 inches long and as big around as your finger. Hold the plant with one hand and pull on the bean with the other.

- The potato plants die. Pull the stems and put them on the compost pile. Then dig around with your hands to find the potatoes. Search wide and deep—potatoes can grow up to 1 foot away from the stem. Spread the potatoes out somewhere sunny and dry (on the ground is OK) for an hour or so, to give them a chance to dry out.

- The peppers are bright orange and the size of a small apple.

- The tomatoes are yellow and soft, but not squishy.

Colorful Crunchers
Medium Recipe

You have never seen a veggie plate that looks like this! Makes snacks for a small group.

Tools

vegetable brush

paper towels

paring knife and cutting board

saucepan

pot holder

big serving basket

Ingredients
From Your Garden

2 orange bell peppers

2 blue potatoes

15 chard leaves

10 radishes

15 tomatoes

20 beans

Steps

1. Make the Rancher Dressing (recipe follows). Chill.

2. Wash all of the vegetables very well. Pat dry on paper towels.

3. Cut the potatoes into circles or sticks $^1/_2$ inch thick. Put potatoes in a saucepan and fill it with water.

4. Boil the potatoes until they are barely tender. Drain and rinse with cold water. Pat dry on paper towels.

5. Cut off the stem end of the peppers and remove the seeds. Cut into circles or strips and remove the white ribs.

6. Cut the chard stems off just below the leaves. Set the leaves aside. Cut the chard stems into 1-inch lengths.

7. Cut the leaves and roots off the radishes.

8. Trim the ends off the beans. If they are long, break them in half.

9. Assemble the basket. First, line it with white napkins. Then line the basket with chard leaves.

10. Place the jar of Rancher Dressing in the basket, with the lid still on.

11. Fill the basket with vegetables, including the chard stems and whole tomatoes. Arrange the veggies to look pretty and show off their colors.

12. When you are ready to serve, remove the lid from the dressing.

Rancher Dressing

The dressing really dresses up a rainbow of vegetables.

Tools

measuring spoons

jar, with lid

measuring cup

Ingredients

From the Market

$^1/_2$ cup mayonnaise or salad dressing

$^1/_2$ cup plain yogurt

$^1/_2$ teaspoon onion, minced

$^1/_4$ teaspoon salt

1 teaspoon dried parsley

$^1/_4$ cup shredded cheddar cheese

Steps

1. Stir together mayonnaise or salad dressing, yogurt, onion powder, salt, and parsley.

2. Chill $^1/_2$ hour.

3. You can experiment with any fresh or dried herb, like dill, basil, or chives. Start with $^1/_4$ teaspoon dried (1 teaspoon fresh) herb and taste before adding more.

4. To make the dressing more colorful, add minced veggies.

Blue and Gold Potato Cakes
Medium Recipe

These aren't your standard flapjacks! Toss out the maple syrup and dig into something different. Makes eight cakes.

Tools

vegetable brush

knife and cutting board

large saucepan

pot holder

measuring cup and spoons

skillet and spatula

ricer or potato masher

mixing spoon

Ingredients
From Your Garden

5 large or 8 medium-size blue potatoes

From the Market

1 stick butter

1 medium-size onion, chopped

1 teaspoon salt

2 tablespoons flour

$1/2$ pound mild cheddar cheese, cut into 8 cubes

Steps

1. Scrub the potatoes and cut them into 1-inch cubes.

2. Fill a saucepan with water and bring to a boil. Add the potatoes and boil until they are tender, 10–15 minutes.

3. While the potatoes are cooking, sauté onion in 4 tablespoons butter until soft.

4. Drain the potatoes and force them through a ricer. Or mash them without adding any water or butter. You want them thick and sticky.

5. Combine onions, salt, flour, and potatoes. Allow the mixture to cool enough to handle.

6. Divide the potatoes into 8 equal cakes.

7. Place a cube of cheese on each cake. Using your hands, form the cakes into balls around the cubes of cheese.

8. Flatten the balls slightly to make thick cakes.

9. Chill the cakes in the refrigerator 15 minutes.

10. Heat remaining butter. Fry potato cakes 4–6 minutes on each side, or until they are well browned and heated through.

Savory Herb Garden
Medium

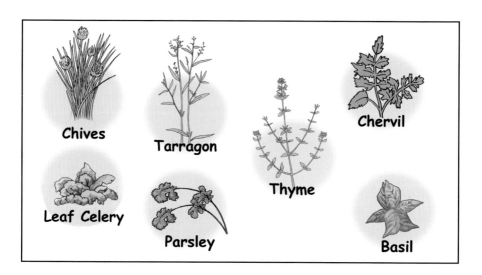

You can use the herbs in this garden to flavor vegetables, meats, stews, salads—even ice cream! Some of the herbs in this garden are perennials. Be sure to plant them in a place where they can grow for a few years.

You Will Need

1 parsley seedling

1 clump chives

1 tarragon seedling

1 dwarf basil seedling

1 thyme seedling

1 package leaf celery seeds

1 package chervil seeds

May I Suggest

Italian (flat-leaved) or Extra Curled Dwarf

French tarragon

Spicy Bush, Purple Ruffles, or Dark Opal

Common thyme or French thyme

Also called smallage, wild celery, cutting celery, soup celery, and seasoning celery. Don't get regular celery—it's not the same thing at all.

Getting Started

- Prepare your soil with extra compost or coarse sand so that it will drain well.

- As soon as the soil is no longer frosty or muddy, plant the chives, parsley, and tarragon.

- Two weeks after the Safe to Plant date, plant the rest of your garden.

- Plant the thyme and tarragon in mounds; plant the rest of the herbs in forts. Page 112 shows you how.

Caring for Your Garden

- Different herbs need different amounts of water. If you water the plants when they droop, you'll be OK.

- Most herbs don't need fertilizer during their first year.

- Pick the flowers off your herbs every day so that the plants will put their energy into leaves, not flowers.

Harvest Your Garden When ...

- The herbs are at least 6–8 inches tall and leafy. Take some of the largest leaves, or pinch off a whole sprig. Be sure to leave plenty of leaves and stems to keep your plants alive!

- In the fall just before the first frost, cut all the herbs down to 2 inches above the ground. After the ground freezes, cover the garden with 6 inches of mulch. Early in the spring, gently rake off the mulch.

Tip
You'll find everything you need to know about planting and caring for your garden in the Green Thumb Guide, starting on page 107.

Many Uses for Savory Herbs
Medium Recipes

Herbs are the "magic secret" to great cooking. Here are four uses for herbs from your garden. Remember to wash them well before you use them.

Bouquet Garni

Steps

1. Gather together 1 sprig thyme, 1 small bunch leaf celery leaves, 1 sprig parsley, and 1 bay leaf.

2. Tie them together with kitchen string.

3. Drop into soups and stews during cooking, or put them inside a whole chicken before you bake it.

4. Remove the bouquet before serving.

Herb-Flavored Ice Cream

Steps

1. Ice cream starts with milk that is heated, then cooled.

2. Drop a handful of herbs or edible flowers into the milk while it is heating.

3. After the milk cools, strain it to remove the flowers or leaves.

4. Basil makes delicious ice cream, and so does lavender. You can find a recipe for ice cream on page 66.

Fines Herbs

Steps

1. Finely snip equal amounts of fresh tarragon, chervil, parsley, and chives.

2. Stir the herbs into soups or stews about 5 minutes before serving.

3. Use about 1 tablespoon of herbs for every 4–6 cups of soup or stew.

Preserving Herbs

Steps

1. Strip leaves off the stems of parsley, basil, and tarragon and freeze in ziplock bags.

2. Hang whole sprigs of thyme upside down. Place in a dark, warm, dry place until the leaves are brittle. Strip leaves off stems and store in opaque containers.

3. Snip or chop chervil leaves into small pieces. Pack tightly into ice cube trays, then fill with water and freeze.

Tip Not all herbs can be preserved, and some lose their flavor very quickly. It's best to use your preserved herbs within a few months after harvesting them.

Three Sisters
Native American Garden
Advanced

Corn, beans, and squash: Each plant helps the others grow. Beans fix nitrogen in the soil, and nitrogen helps corn grow. Squash covers the ground like mulch, and the prickly vines keep animals from raiding your garden. This garden draws on the tradition of the Wampanoag nation. A Wampanoag man, Squanto, taught the Pilgrims to farm corn and other native plants.

**Three Sisters
Native American Garden Plot**

You Will Need

1 package of corn seeds

1 package of pinto or kidney bean seeds (ask for low-growing bush beans)

1 package of acorn squash seeds (if your growing season is short, use seedlings)

May I Suggest

Use native plant seeds from:

Native Seeds/Search
2509 N. Campbell Avenue, #345
Tucson, AZ 85719

Tip This garden will not work in containers.

Getting Started

- In this garden, seeds are planted in mounds. When you are ready to plant, put a stick or rock every 4 feet to mark the center of each mound you are going to make.

- Make mounds by gathering up dirt into big, flat piles about 4 inches tall. Create corn/bean mounds about 2 feet across. Make squash mounds 1 foot across.

- Make a small fort at the top of each mound or a moat around the bottom of it. Page 112 shows you how.

- Start two weeks after your Safe to Plant date. The chart on page 6 shows the Safe to Plant date for your region.

 Tip Soak your corn and bean seeds in warm water for a few hours before you plant to make them sprout faster.

- Plant six corn seeds in the top of each corn/bean mound. Wait two or three weeks, until the corn is as tall as your finger.

- Pull up the two smallest corn plants from each mound and throw them on the compost heap.

Tip If your garden is very small, you can plant just one mound with corn, beans, and squash. Make the mound about 3 feet across.

- Then plant the beans and squash.

Caring for Your Garden

- Corn needs lots of water and fertilizer. Water your garden at least twice a week, mulch it with compost, and give it a big drink of garden tea every other week.

- Page 123 shows you how to make garden tea.

- Don't mulch—the big leaves on your squash plants will do that job.

- When the corn is a few feet tall, pack some dirt around the bottom of each stalk. This will help the corn stand up straight when the beans begin to climb.

- If the beans start to smother the corn, trim the bean vines a little or pull them off the cornstalks. That will give the corn a chance to grow a little taller before the beans start climbing again.

Harvest Your Garden When ...

- The corn is juicy and the silks are brown and dry. Peel back a little of the husk and poke one of the kernels with your fingernail. If a milky liquid comes out, the corn is ready. If the liquid is clear and watery, the corn is not ripe yet. (Close the husks and wait a few weeks, then try again.) If the corn is tough and dry, it is old.

- The beans pods are brown and dry. Spread the pods on an old sheet in a warm, dry place and leave them for a few days to be sure they are completely dry. Then break open the pods and take the beans out.

- The acorn squash has a very hard shell. It will be dark green and orange. Use pruning shears to cut the stem a few inches above the squash. This is a job for an adult.

Three Sisters Supper
Advanced Recipe

This is a basic recipe using foods common to many Native American groups.

Tools

large knife

baking dish

pot holder

meat fork

tablespoon

table knife or pastry brush (for spreading butter)

covered baking dish

saucepan with lid

colander

ladle

Ingredients

From Your Garden

1 medium-size acorn squash

2 ears of corn

$1/2$ cup beans, shelled

From the Market

2 tablespoons butter

salt and pepper

Steps

1. Wash the squash.

2. Have an adult pierce it several times with a large knife.

3. Place the squash in a baking pan and bake it at 375 degrees Fahrenheit until you can easily pierce it with the meat fork. A small squash will take 45 minutes; larger squashes take longer.

4. Remove the squash from the oven and reduce the heat to 250 degrees Fahrenheit.

5. Have an adult cut the squash in half and scrape out the seeds and strings.

6. Now you have two squash bowls. Brush the inside of each bowl with 1 tablespoon butter. Sprinkle with salt and pepper. Put the squash bowls in a covered casserole in the oven.

7. While the squash is cooking, boil the beans in plenty of water until they are soft. These beans are fresh, not dried, so they should cook in about 30 to 45 minutes.

8. Drain the beans in the colander, then return them to the pan and keep them warm over low heat.

9. Season them with salt and pepper. If you like, add a can of diced green chiles.

10. Shuck and clean the corn, then cook it according to the directions on pages 52–53.

11. Remove the squash bowls from the oven. Ladle some beans into each squash bowl. Serve with hot corn on the cob.

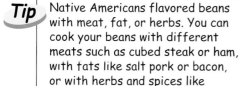 **Tip** Native Americans flavored beans with meat, fat, or herbs. You can cook your beans with different meats such as cubed steak or ham, with fats like salt pork or bacon, or with herbs and spices like oregano and chili powder.

Stir-Fry Garden
Medium

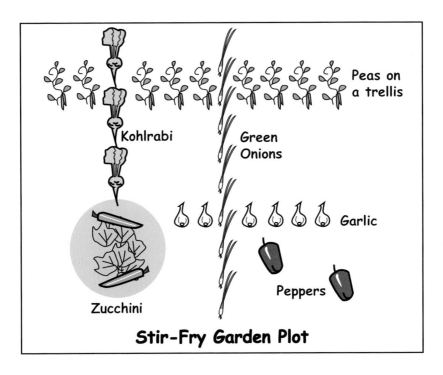

Stir-Fry Garden Plot

Peas on a trellis

Kohlrabi

Green Onions

Garlic

Zucchini

Peppers

The surprise in this garden is kohlrabi. It's a fun plant that grows fast, doesn't take much work, and looks very odd. Some people say it looks like a spaceship. Kohlrabi has a light, mild flavor.

You Will Need

1 package edible-pod pea seeds
2 red bell pepper seedling
1 package zucchini seeds
1 package kohlrabi seeds
1 green onion set
1 garlic set

May I Suggest

Dwarf Gray Sugar
Earlired
Aristocrat or Gold Rush

Tip Soak the peas in warm water for a few hours before you plant to make them sprout faster.

Getting Started

- As soon as the ground is no longer frosty or muddy, plant kohlrabi, onions, garlic, and peas.

- Peas are climbers. Plant them near a sturdy chain-link fence or in cages. Page 23 shows you how.

- Two weeks after the Safe to Plant date, plant the zucchini and peppers.

- The chart on page 6 shows the Safe to Plant date for your region.

Caring for Your Garden

- Kohlrabi, zucchini, peppers, and peas need lots of water. Keep the soil around them damp all the time.

- Garlic and onions need less water. Water them only when the soil around them is dry.

- Thin the kohlrabi, but not the peas.

- If your zucchini plants wilt, you may have borers. Page 120 shows you what to do.

Harvest Your Garden When ...

- The kohlrabi bulbs are 1–2 inches across. Cut the stem 1 inch above the bulb.

- The green onions are at least 6 inches tall. Pick every second onion in a row. That will give the onions you leave behind more room to grow.

- The garlic stems fall over and die. Dig the garlic up with your hands so that you don't hurt the bulb.

- The pea pods are small and flat and the peas are just tiny bumps.

- The zucchini are about 5 inches long.

- The peppers are bright red and the size of a small apple.

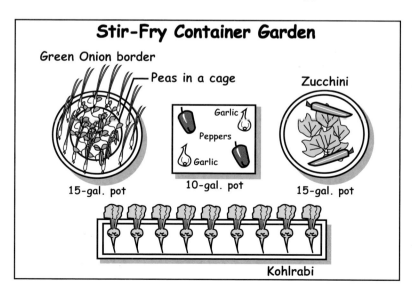

Stir-Fry Container Garden

Green Onion border

Peas in a cage

Zucchini

Garlic

Peppers

Garlic

15-gal. pot

10-gal. pot

15-gal. pot

Kohlrabi

Garden Lo Mein
Medium Recipe

Stir-fries have lots of ingredients, tools, and steps, but all the steps are easy and quick. Line up everything you need before you start, and you will be amazed how quickly it all comes together! Adults should handle the stir-frying. Makes six servings.

Tools

vegetable brush

bowls or plates for holding each ingredient

knife and cutting board

measuring cup and spoons

grater

can opener

saucepan

pot holders

mixing spoon

small cup

large pot for cooking noodles

skillet or wok

spatula

ovenproof serving dish

Ingredients

From Your Garden

2 green onions, thinly sliced

1 clove garlic, minced

1 zucchini, grated

2 kohlrabi, peeled and chopped

1 red bell pepper, chopped

15 pea pods

From the Market

2 tablespoons dark soy sauce

$1/2$ cup plus 3 tablespoons chicken stock

1 tablespoon cornstarch

$1/2$ pound lo mein noodles

3 tablespoons peanut oil

2 slices ginger root, peeled and minced

$1/2$ teaspoon sugar

$1/2$ cup mung bean sprouts (page 42 shows you how to grow sprouts)

1 cup cooked pork or chicken, shredded

Steps

1. Heat the oven to 250 degrees Fahrenheit.

2. In a saucepan, combine the soy sauce and stock.

3. In a small cup, combine the cornstarch with 1 tablespoon water.

4. Cook noodles according to directions on package. Drain and rinse with cold water.

WARNING
Stir frying should be done by experienced adults only.

5. Heat wok or large skillet over high heat for 30 seconds. Add $1^1/_2$ tablespoons peanut oil and heat for 20 seconds more.

6. Add noodles and stir fry 3–4 minutes. Avoid any splattering oil!

7. Empty contents of wok into ovenproof serving dish and keep warm, uncovered, in oven set at 250 degrees Fahrenheit.

8. Set soy sauce mixture over high heat. When it starts to boil, remove saucepan from heat.

Tip In China, noodles are traditionally served on birthdays. The long noodles are not cut because they symbolize long life.

9. Heat $1^1/_2$ tablespoons peanut oil in the wok over high heat. Stir-fry the green onions, garlic, ginger, zucchini, red bell pepper, kohlrabi, and pea pods 2–3 minutes.

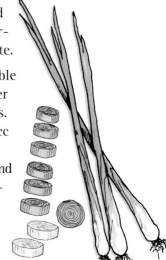

10. Add the sugar and the boiling soy sauce mixture. Bring it to a boil again.

11. Stir the cornstarch mixture and then add it to the vegetables. Also add the bean sprouts and meat. Stir-fry 1 minute.

12. Put vegetable stir-fry over the noodles. Toss it twice to make it look nice and serve immediately.

It's-Not-Spaghetti Garden
Advanced

It's-Not-Spaghetti Garden Plot

When is spaghetti not spaghetti? When it's a squash! Spaghetti squash grows like a squash and it looks like a squash, but when you cut it open you will find long, pale strands that look like spaghetti.

You Will Need

	May I Suggest
1 package carrot seeds	Any short carrot (check the seed packet), like Nantes or Little Finger
several cloves of garlic	
2 parsley seedlings	Italian flat parsley
1 bush basil seedling	Spicy Globe or Greek Mini
2 bell pepper seedlings	Earlired or California Wonder
1 package spaghetti squash seeds	Pasta Hybrid (for pots)
1 package yellow summer squash seeds	Yellow Crookneck or Gold Rush (zucchini)

May I Suggest

Getting Started

- As soon as the ground is no longer frosty or muddy, plant your carrots, parsley, and garlic.

- For the carrots, loosen the soil 6–8 inches deep. This will give your carrots room to grow.

- Two weeks after the Safe to Plant date, plant the rest of your garden.

- The chart on page 6 shows the Safe to Plant date for your region.

Caring for Your Garden

- Most of the plants in this garden love water. Garlic likes a little less water.

- If your squash plants wilt, you may have borers. Page 120 shows you what to do.

- Pick the flowers off your basil every day so that the plant will put its energy into leaves, not flowers.

Harvest Your Garden When ...

- The carrots are at least $1/2$ inch across and start to peek through the dirt. Pull up the ones with the largest tops first.

- The garlic stems fall over and die. Dig the garlic up with your hands so that you don't hurt the bulb.

- The parsley and basil are 4–6 inches tall and leafy. Take the largest leaves, or pinch off a whole sprig. Leave plenty of green leaves and stems to keep your plants alive!

- The peppers are bright red and the size of a small apple. Cut the stem about 1 inch above the pepper.

- The spaghetti squash after the first frost, when the shell is so hard you can't cut it with your thumbnail, even if you push very hard. Use pruning shears to cut the stem a few inches above the squash. This is a job for an adult.

- The summer squash are about as long as your hand, from fingertip to wrist.

It's-Not-Spaghetti Container Garden

Spaghetti Squash
Garlic
Parsley
Basil
Summer Squash
Peppers
Garlic
15-gal. pot
15-gal. container
15-gal. pot
Carrots   10-inches deep

It's-Not-Pasta Primavera
Advanced Recipe

This recipe uses everything your garden has to offer. Makes eight servings.

Tools

vegetable brush

paring knife and cutting board

measuring cup and spoons

grater

scissors

9-x-13-inch baking pan

pot holder

meat fork

large sharp knife

table fork

2 large, ovenproof, covered casseroles

2 serving spoons

skillet

mixing spoon

large saucepan

Ingredients
From Your Garden

1 spaghetti squash

2 cloves garlic, smashed and peeled

1 summer squash, thinly sliced

1 red pepper, diced

1 cup carrot, grated

$1/4$ cup parsley, finely minced

$1/4$ cup basil, finely minced

From the Market

$1/2$ teaspoon black pepper

5 $1/2$ tablespoons butter

3 tablespoons flour

1 cup milk, warmed

1 cup chicken stock or canned broth

$1/2$ teaspoon salt (leave this out if you use canned broth)

$1/4$ cup freshly grated Parmesan cheese

 Tip You can make the sauce using a mix, like Knorr's Red Pepper Pesto Sauce, or a bottled Alfredo sauce. Just follow the package directions in place of steps 9–15 here.
This recipe is great with cooked, cubed chicken or turkey tossed in.

Steps

1. Bake the *whole, uncut* spaghetti squash in the baking pan at 350 degrees Fahrenheit.

2. After 1¼ hours, poke the squash with the meat fork to see if it is tender. If it is not, continue to bake, checking every 15 minutes, until it is done.

3. Remove the spaghetti squash from the oven. Lower the oven temperature to 200 degrees Fahrenheit.

4. Have an adult cut the spaghetti squash in half lengthwise and remove the seeds.

5. Have an adult use a fork to scrape out the flesh. It will fall away in long strands, like spaghetti.

6. Put the spaghetti squash strands in a large baking dish and toss with 1 tablespoon butter. Cover the dish and place in the oven to keep warm.

7. In the skillet, sauté the garlic in 2 tablespoons butter for 1 minute. Add the summer squash, pepper, and carrots and sauté 3 minutes more.

8. Stir in the parsley, basil, and black pepper. Put into a baking dish, cover, and put it in the oven to keep warm.

9. To prepare the sauce, melt 2½ tablespoons butter over medium heat in the saucepan. Add the flour and stir briskly to make a smooth paste. (The paste is called a roux.)

10. Cook the roux, stirring constantly, until it is golden.

11. Add 1 tablespoon of broth to the roux, then stir until the liquid is completely absorbed. Do this with all of the broth—1 tablespoon at a time.

12. Then add the milk slowly, stirring constantly. Take it slow, and you won't have any lumps.

13. Simmer the sauce 5–10 minutes, stirring constantly. Don't let it boil.

14. Lower the heat to the lowest setting.

15. Add the cheese and stir until it melts.

16. Pour the sauce over the veggie mixture. Toss gently with two large spoons until all the vegetables are coated with the sauce.

17. Fluff up the spaghetti squash.

18. Spread the vegetable and sauce mixture over it, then toss the whole thing once or twice to make it look nice. Serve immediately.

Basil Bob's Vegetable Garden
Advanced

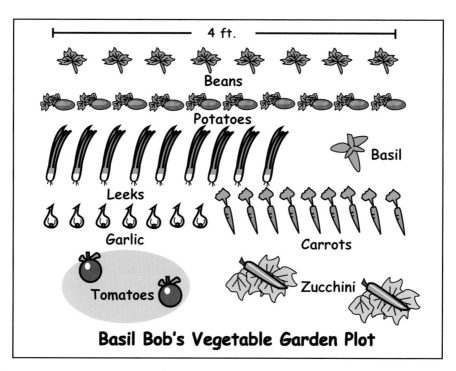

4 ft.	
Beans	
Potatoes	
Leeks	Basil
Garlic	Carrots
Tomatoes	Zucchini

Basil Bob's Vegetable Garden Plot

You can take one cup of every vegetable that is ready to harvest, combine them with a few ingredients from the market—and voila! Soup!

Tip Leeks take a long time to mature. Don't plant them if your growing season is less than 130 days. (Ask a clerk at your garden center how long your season is.)

Getting Started

- As soon as the soil is no longer frosty or muddy, plant your leeks, carrots, garlic, and potatoes.

- Plant the leeks in trenches—rows that are 6 inches wide and 10 inches deep.

You Will Need

1 package leek seeds . . . .

1 package carrot seeds . . . .

several cloves of garlic

10 seed potatoes . . . .

1 package snap or bush green bean seeds . . .

2 tomato plants . . . .

1 basil seedling . . . .

1 package zucchini seeds . . . .

May I Suggest

Titan or Large American Flag

Any 4- to 5-inch carrot (check the
   seed packet for size)

Red Pontiac

Bush Blue Lake

Early Girl for gardens, Pixie for pots

Spicy Bush or Dark Opal

Aristocrat (green) or Gold Rush
   (yellow)

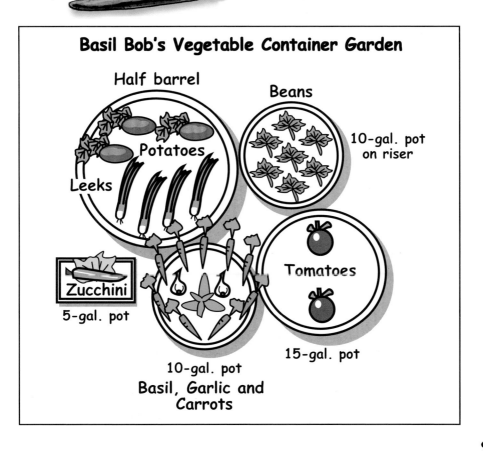

Basil Bob's Vegetable Container Garden

Half barrel

Beans

Potatoes

Leeks

10-gal. pot
on riser

Zucchini

5-gal. pot

Tomatoes

15-gal. pot

10-gal. pot
Basil, Garlic and
Carrots

- Dig to loosen the soil about 6 inches deep for the carrots and about 18 inches deep for the potatoes. This will give your plants room to grow.

Use seed potatoes; or use potatoes from the grocery store cut into four pieces, making sure each piece has at least two eyes. Let the potato pieces dry out for two days before you plant them. Plant the potatoes 4 inches deep.

- After your Safe to Plant date, plant the beans.

- Two weeks after your Safe to Plant date, plant the tomatoes, zucchini, and basil. The chart on page 6 shows the Safe to Plant date for your region.

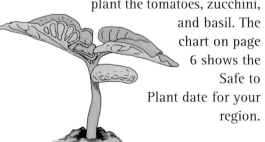

Caring for Your Garden

- Zucchini like lots of water. Always keep the soil around them damp. The other plants need less water; water them deeply but less often.

- When potatoes and leeks are about 6 inches tall, pile up about 1 inch of dirt around them. Be sure to get the dirt right up against the stems. Do this once a week until harvest.

- If your zucchini plants wilt, you may have borers. Page 120 shows you what to do.

- Pick the flowers off your basil every day so that the plant will put its energy into leaves, not flowers.

Harvest Your Garden When ...

- The leeks are about $1/2$ to 1 inch across. Dig them out with a shovel, root and all.

Spread them out somewhere sunny and dry for an hour or so. Then cut off the root.

- The carrots start to peek through the dirt.

- The garlic stems fall over and die. Dig the garlic up with your hands so that you don't hurt the bulb.

- The potatoes' leaves and stems die. Pull the stems and put them on the compost heap. Then dig around with your hands to find the potatoes. Search wide and deep—potatoes can grow up to 1 foot away from the stem. Spread them out somewhere sunny and dry (on the ground is OK) for an hour or so, to give them a chance to dry out.

- The beans are 3–4 inches long and as big around as your finger.

- The tomatoes are red and soft, but not squishy.

- The zucchini are about 5 inches long.

- The basil is at least 4 inches tall and leafy. Leave plenty of green leaves and stems to keep your plants alive!

WARNING

Flowers will form and fall off your potato plants. Then fruit will form on the plants. Don't eat the fruit— it is poisonous. The potatoes are tubers—they grow underground.

Basil Bob's 1–Cup Vegetable Soup
Advanced Recipe

Homemade soup is warm and homey; that's why it's called "comfort food." Serve it with your own Best Bread (page 44) and comfort eight hungry people!

Tools

vegetable brush

paring knife and cutting board

can opener

measuring cup and spoons

paper towels

large bowl

large soup pot with cover

pot holder

mixing spoon

Ingredients
From Your Garden

1 clove garlic, smashed and peeled

2 leeks

2 large tomatoes, peeled, seeded, and chopped

3 small red-skinned potatoes, scrubbed and diced

2 large carrots (or 4 small ones), scrubbed and sliced

handfuls of green beans, scrubbed and broken into 1-inch lengths

1 zucchini, washed and diced

as many basil leaves as you can pack into 1 cup

From the Market

4 tablespoons butter, divided

one 1-pound can small white beans

3 cups chicken broth

pepper

1/2 cup raw macaroni (or spaghetti broken into 1/2-inch pieces)

Tip You should have about 1 cup of each kind of vegetable. If you have more veggies than you need, save them to make a salad or another soup.

Steps

1. Remove the tough outer layer or two from each leek.

2. Cut off the dark green tops where they begin to separate into leaves.

3. Lay a leek on the cutting board and cut it in half the long way. Then slice it to make thin half-moons. Do this to all the leeks.

4. Put the pieces in a big bowl of cool water and rub them vigorously between your hands to separate the layers and get all the dirt out. Empty the water and do it again.

5. Keep washing and rinsing until there are no bits of dirt hiding in the leeks.

6. Warm 2 tablespoons of butter in the large soup pot over medium heat.

7. Add the leeks and one clove of garlic. Stir.

8. Add the tomatoes. Stir and cook for 5 minutes.

9. Add the potatoes, carrots, green beans, and white beans. Then add the broth, 3 cups cold water, 2 tablespoons of butter, and two shakes of pepper.

10. Bring to a boil. Turn the heat down, cover the pot, and simmer for 10 minutes.

11. Add the zucchini, pasta, and basil. Simmer 20 more minutes.

12. Remove the soup from the heat. Serve right away.

Tip You can "mess around" with this recipe: Try red beans instead of white ones, or beef broth instead of chicken. Add corn or peas—whatever you like!

The A-maze-ing, Never-Ending Salad Garden
Advanced

This big garden has everything you need to make all kinds of salads in spring, summer, and fall. To care for your plants, work your way through the maze.

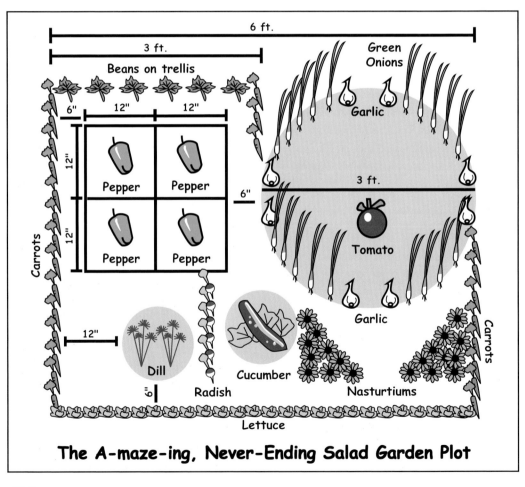

The A-maze-ing, Never-Ending Salad Garden Plot

You Will Need

2 packages leaf lettuce seeds · · · · · · · · ·

3 packages carrot seeds · · · · · · · · · · ·

several cloves of garlic

1 package radish seeds · · · · · · · · · · · ·

1 package bush snap bean seeds · · · · · ·

2 dill seedlings · · · · · · · · · · · · · · · · ·

1 tomato seedling · · · · · · · · · · · · · · · ·

1 onion set

4 pepper seedlings · · · · · · · · · · · · · · ·

2 packages nasturtium seeds

1 cucumber seedling · · · · · · · · · · · · · ·

May I Suggest

Red Sails or Salad Bowl

Nantes (straight) and Orbit or
Thumbelina (round)

Cherry Belle or Easter Egg

Bush Blue Lake

Dill Bouquet is good for pots

Early Girl, Red Cherry, or Super
Sweet 100 (Pixie for pots)

California Wonder (bell peppers) or
Jingle Bells (tiny sweet peppers)

Bush Champion for gardens; Salad
Bush Hybrid for pots

Getting Started

- As soon as the ground is no longer frosty or muddy, plant your lettuce, carrots, radishes, garlic, and onions.

- For the carrots and garlic, dig around in the soil to loosen it 6 inches deep. This will give your plants room to grow.

- After your Safe to Plant date, plant the beans, dill, and nasturtiums.

- Two weeks after the Safe to Plant date, plant the rest of your garden.

- The chart on page 6 shows the Safe to Plant date for your region.

Tip Soak your bean seeds in warm water for a few hours before you plant to make them sprout faster.

Caring for Your Garden

- Peppers, lettuce, cucumbers, carrots, nasturtiums, radishes, and dill love water. Tomatoes, beans, onions, and garlic need a little less water.

- Lettuce needs lots of fertilizer. Give it a drink of garden tea every other week. Be sure to pour the tea on the ground, not on the plant.

- You don't need to thin leaf lettuce; harvesting will do the job.

- You can grow cucumbers and tomatoes on stakes or in cages to make them stand up straight and take

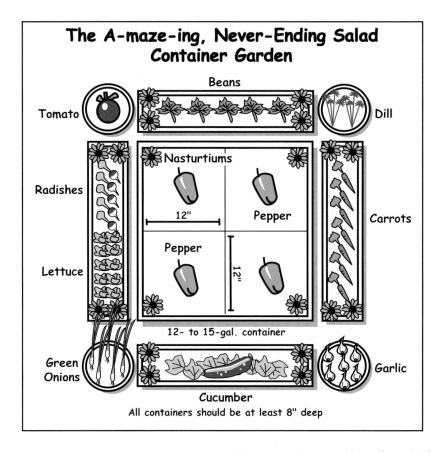

The A-maze-ing, Never-Ending Salad Container Garden

Tomato

Beans

Dill

Radishes

Nasturtiums

12"

Pepper

Pepper

12"

Carrots

Lettuce

12- to 15-gal. container

Green Onions

Cucumber

Garlic

All containers should be at least 8" deep

up less room in the garden. Buy a cage from a garden center or use a sturdy dowel (5 feet long). Page 23 tells how to use a cage. Page 27 tells how to use a stake.

- It is OK for dill to turn yellow after it has been growing awhile.

- If a cucumber's leaves wilt, it probably has a disease. Dig up the whole plant and throw it in the trash.

- Some of these plants might attract bugs. Pages 118–121 show you what to do about them.

Harvest Your Garden When …

- The lettuce is 3 or 4 inches tall. Pick all the leaves that are more than 3 inches tall.

- The carrots and radishes are about $^1/_2$ inch across. Pick the ones with the biggest tops first. Keep harvesting until the radishes and carrots are 1 inch across.

- The garlic stems fall over and die in the fall. Dig the garlic up with your hands so that you don't hurt the bulb. Dry it by laying it on a screen for a few hours in a warm, shady, dry place.

- The green onions are at least 6 inches tall.

- The beans are 3–4 inches long and as big around as your finger. Hold the plant with one hand and pull on the bean with the other.

- The nasturtiums have plenty of leaves. Pick off the smallest leaves and freshest flowers.

- The dill is at least 6 inches tall and leafy. Take the largest leaves, or pinch off a whole sprig. Leave plenty of green leaves and stems to keep your plants alive!

- The tomatoes are red and soft, but not squishy.

- The bell peppers are bright green and about the size of an apple. If you leave them on the plant longer, they will turn red and sweet. Cut the stem about an inch above the pepper.

- The cucumbers are about 6 inches long. Cut or twist the cucumber off the stem.

Tip After you harvest the lettuce and radishes, you will have some holes in your maze. Plug the holes by planting more carrots for a fall harvest.

The Never-Ending Salad Bar
Easy Recipes

You can make a salad out of whatever is ready to harvest. There is always something new you can do. Here are a few ideas.

Spring Salad

Steps

1. Toss 1 cup of lettuce leaves, 3 chopped radishes, and 8 nasturtium flowers with a light vinaigrette dressing.

2. Light vinaigrette: 2 tablespoons pale olive oil, 1 tablespoon lemon juice, $1/4$ teaspoon sugar.

Early Summer Salad

Steps

1. Arrange 8 snap beans, 2 carrots cut into sticks, 2 green onions, and 1 boiled egg cut into fourths the long way, on a plate.

2. Decorate with nasturtium flowers and serve with Rancher Dressing (see page 76).

Midsummer Salad

Steps

1. Chop 1 large tomato (or small tomatoes or 8 cherry tomatoes), 1 cucumber, and the white parts of 2 green onions.

2. Combine with 2 cups cooked cold macaroni.

3. Dress with Dilly Dressing and sprinkle with green onion confetti (see page 37).

Dilly Dressing

Steps

1. Mix together $1/2$ cup mayonnaise or salad dressing, 2 tablespoons apple cider vinegar, 1 tablespoon minced dill leaves, and 2 shakes of white pepper.

2. If you use regular white vinegar, which is very strong, add 1 teaspoon sugar.

Fall Salad

Steps

1. Combine 1 cup finely grated carrot, 1 tablespoon raisins, and 1 tablespoon chopped walnuts (optional).

2. Mix with Spice Dressing.

Christmas in July Salad

Steps

1. Cut the tops off 2 red peppers and 2 green peppers.

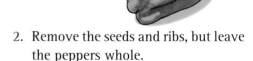

2. Remove the seeds and ribs, but leave the peppers whole.

3. Combine $1^1/2$ cups cold cooked rice, $1/2$ cup cold cooked shredded chicken, $1/4$ cup grated cheddar cheese, $1/4$ cup chopped tomato, and 1 small chopped cucumber.

4. Make dressing with 1 cup yogurt, 2 teaspoons milk, 1 teaspoon honey, 1 pinch of dried mustard, $1/2$ teaspoon prepared yellow mustard, and one shake each of salt and pepper.

5. Mix the dressing with the rice, then stuff it into the peppers.

Spice Dressing

Steps

1. Combine $1/4$ cup mayonnaise or yogurt and 1 teaspoon cinnamon, and tiny pinch of nutmeg.

I'm Dreaming of a _____ Garden
Advanced

Design your own garden! Start by thinking about what you like to eat—that's your Dream Dish. Then follow these five easy steps to creating your own Dream Garden.

Steps

1. Pick a recipe you really like. Cookbooks with great recipes are listed in the bibliography (page 127).

2. List all the ingredients that go in or with your favorite recipe.

3. Draw a star next to the ingredients that you can grow. If there are lots of them, pick four or five that you want to grow.

4. Sketch a garden plan to show where you will plant your plants. You can make your garden a basic square or a unique shape: a wagon wheel, a

 Tip It is best if all the vegetables are ready to harvest at the same time. Cool crops, like peas and radishes, will be long gone by the time warm-weather crops, like tomatoes and melons, are ready to harvest. Ask an experienced gardener or a clerk at your local gardening store to help you choose which vegetables to plant. Or read seed packets to be sure all your vegetables have about the same number of "Days to Harvest."

Tip Make it pretty! Tuck flowers in your garden's nooks and crannies to make it look nice.

clock, a ladder, interlocking circles, or even your initials!

5. The plans in this book and your seed packets will give you an idea how far apart to space your plants. Or you can look in a good gardening book, like *The Victory Garden Kids' Book* (for garden spots) or *Movable Harvests* (for container gardens). The only other thing to remember is to put the tall plants in a row along the north side of the garden so that they don't cast shadows on the rest of the plants.

Sketching the Garden Plan

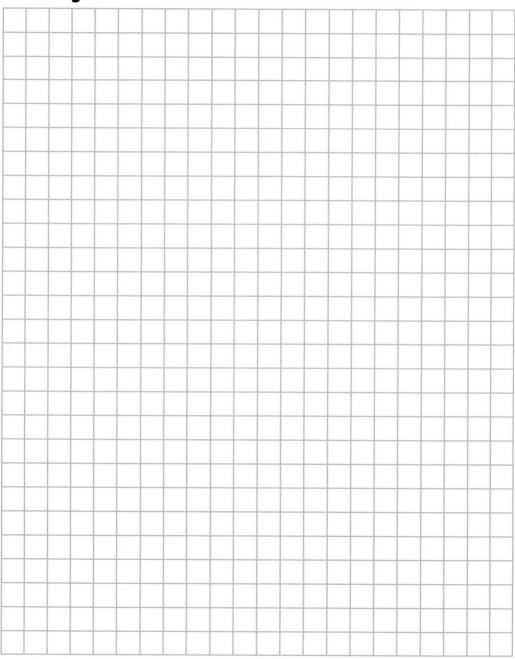

Green Thumb Guide
Getting Started

Your Soil Is Ready to Work When ...

- It is no longer frozen or muddy. Pick up a handful of dirt and look at it. If you see frost or ice crystals, it's *way* too early to work. Squeeze the dirt *hard*. If muddy water oozes out between your fingers, the soil is too wet.

- If you test your soil and it is too frosty or muddy to work, wait a week or two and try again.

Preparing Your Soil
... in the Garden

As soon as the soil is ready to work, you can start adding nutrients and other good stuff. Here's what to do:

1. Dig around in the dirt to loosen it. Just dig up a shovelful of dirt, then turn it over and let the dirt fall back on the ground. Loosen the soil down to 10 inches deep.

2. Test your soil's pH. It's a quick and easy test, and you can buy the kit at any garden center. The test will give you a pH number for your soil. A good number is 6. If your soil's pH is below 5.5 or above 7, ask the people at the garden center what you need to do to fix it. They will give you some powder (limestone or agricultural sulfur) to sprinkle on your soil. Let an adult do this.

Tip Anything that will hold dirt and water will hold a plant. Try an old bathtub, four stacked-up tires, a laundry basket lined with a garbage bag, a trunk, or even a baby carriage!

3. While you are at the garden center, buy 40 pounds of compost, 20 pounds of manure, and ¹/₂ bale of peat moss.

Tip If your yard doesn't already have a garden space, you can tuck your vegetables in flower beds or use containers.

4. Mix them together and spread the mix over the garden to make a layer 3 inches deep. (Mix up a second batch if you need it.)

5. Stir the soil with a shovel until everything is mixed together. Smooth the garden with the back of a metal rake, if you have one, or with your hands.

... in Pots

You can mix soil with an equal amount of compost to use in pots. Or you can make a super soil mix by combining:

1. 5 gallons aged compost with manure

2. 1 gallon coarse sand

3. 1 gallon vermiculite or perlite (available in garden centers)

4. 1 gallon ground-up spahgnum peat moss

Fill each container with soil/compost or super soil mix, and you're ready to plant!

Tip Carving a garden out of a lawn is a *lot* of work, even for adults. When you're ready for the challenge, you can find instructions for creating a garden plot in *The Victory Garden Kids' Book*.

Planting
Hardening Off

Take your seedlings outside every day for two weeks so that they can get used to the sun and wind. During the first week, put them in a protected place where they won't get too much sun or wind. During the second week, set them out right where you are going to plant them.

Rows, Beds, and Mounds

You can plant in rows, beds, or mounds. Mounds are good if your soil tends to be soggy.

- To plant in rows, draw a line in the dirt with your finger and plant inside the line.

- To plant in beds, draw a big square in the dirt with your finger. Scatter seeds over the whole square.

- To plant in mounds, pile dirt in a circle and flatten the top of it. Plant your seeds or seedlings in a circle around the top of the mound.

Seeds

The seed packet will tell you:

- when to plant

- whether to plant in rows, beds, or mounds

- how deep to plant your seeds

- how far apart to space them

Tip
To make big, hard seeds (like peas and beans) sprout faster, soak them in warm water for an hour before you plant.

To Plant Seeds

1. Read the seed packet.

2. Make your row, bed, or mound.

3. Press large seeds into the dirt, one by one. Close up the hole with dirt and press gently to set the seed in place. If the seeds are too tiny to drop one by one, take a pinch between your thumb and finger and sprinkle the seeds where you want them to grow. Then sprinkle dirt over the seeds to cover them and press gently to set the seeds in place.

4. Water: Remember, seeds need just a little water all the time. Water them once a day—or twice a day if the soil is dry. The soil should feel like a washcloth that has been wrung out.

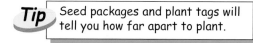

To Plant Seedlings

1. Make rows, beds, or mounds. Water the soil lightly.

2. Set your seedlings on the dirt where you are going to plant them.

3. Use your hands or a trowel to dig a hole just a little bigger than the seedling's container.

4. Using your thumbs, press gently on the bottom of the seedling's container to push the plant up and out. Do not tug on the seedling.

Tip
Seed packages and plant tags will tell you how far apart to plant.

5. Set the plant in the planting hole. Check to be sure the crown (where the roots meet the stem) is at ground level. If it's too low, put a little dirt in the bottom of the hole. If it's too high, take a little dirt out of the hole.

6. Push soil down into the hole around the roots of the plant. Push gently to be sure there are no empty spaces. Then press down on the soil surface *gently* to set the plant in place.

7. Put a cutworm collar around every seedling. You can make the collars out of paper cups (or toilet paper holders or even milk cartons).

To Plant Bulbs

1. Make rows, beds, or mounds. Water the soil lightly.

2. Place the bulbs where you are going to plant them.

3. Push the bulb down into the ground until just the tip shows.

4. Water lightly.

Tip Don't worry if your seeds don't sprout or your seedlings die. Gardening takes practice, and every gardener has trouble from time to time. You can start over with new seeds and plants, or you can focus on growing what *did* come up for you.

Forts and Moats

Build forts or moats around your plants to hold the water near their roots. Forts work for plants that need lots of water all the time. You can fill the fort with mulch and water right on top of the mulch. Make the walls of the fort a few inches tall to hold the mulch and water. Some plants that like lots of water are lettuce, radishes, carrots, kohlrabi, basil, summer squash, and cucumbers.

Moats direct water away from plants. This forces plants to grow long, healthy roots. Make your moats a few inches deep. This works especially well for tomatoes, peppers, winter squash, and most herbs.

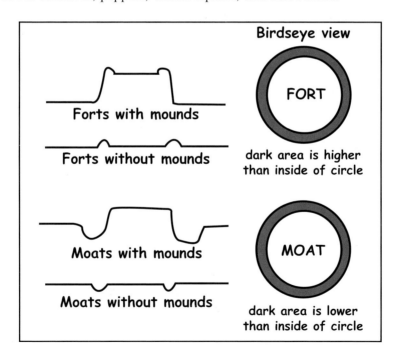

Birdseye view

Forts with mounds

Forts without mounds

FORT

dark area is higher than inside of circle

Moats with mounds

Moats without mounds

MOAT

dark area is lower than inside of circle

Watering

How to Water Your New Garden

Water all your seeds and seedlings right after you plant them. Use a gentle sprinkle from a watering can or a hose with a sprinkler attachment. Water slowly and gently, wagging the water back and forth over the row, until you see puddles. Wait until the puddles disappear, then water again.

Keep the soil over your seeds damp (but not muddy) all the time. Seeds will rot if they get too wet, and they will die if they get dry.

Check the soil each morning and evening, and water lightly whenever it is dusty dry. After a few weeks, when the seeds sprout and your seedlings are used to their new home, you can cut back on the water.

When to Water

You and Mother Nature can work together to water your garden. When it rains a lot, you don't need to water. When it rains a little, water once a week. When it's hot and dry or windy, you might need to water two or three times a week.

There are two easy ways to tell when your plants need water:

1. To check the soil around your plants' roots, stick your finger in the soil until it is buried up to your knuckle. Now pull out your finger. If some damp dirt sticks to your finger, your plant is OK. If the dirt on the tip of your finger is dusty, your plant needs water.

2. Check your plants first thing in the morning. The ones that are drooping need water. (Most plants droop during the heat of the day, so be sure to check them in the morning.)

How to Water

Take it slow, and do it twice. To water rows and beds, use a watering can with a sprinkler rose or a sprinkler head on a hose. Let the water run slowly as you wag the watering can or hose back and forth across the row or bed. Water until puddles form. Stop. Wait for the puddles to seep into the soil, then water again. If you have moats or forts, slowly fill them with water. Wait until the water seeps into the soil, then do it again.

To water the whole garden at once, set up a lawn sprinkler to cover the whole garden. Turn the water on until puddles *begin* to form, then turn it off for 15 minutes, then turn it on again until puddles begin to form. Do this early in the morning. Plants suffer if their leaves are wet during the afternoon or at night.

Containers

Soil in pots dries out fast. Water the pots every day—even twice a day in hot weather. The secret to watering pots is: Water twice. Run the water slowly and gently until all the dirt is wet and the water runs out the bottom of the pot. Wait a few minutes, then do it again. The first time gets the soil wet enough to hold water. The second watering really gets the job done.

Thinning Your Plants

When you plant small seeds, the plants end up too close together. The seed packet tells you how far apart the plants should be after you thin them. All you do is pick the sprouts that are crowding their neighbors. Thinning is easy: Put one hand on the ground around the "keeper" plant to hold it in place while you pick the plants that are crowding it. Try to pick the smaller sprouts and leave the bigger ones. You can eat thinnings of lettuce, carrots, and radishes.

Tip Even plants in containers need thinning!

Feeding

It takes food to make food. And most plants are *big* eaters. You can help your plants grow bigger and stronger by feeding them really good food all summer long. You can mulch with compost mixed with manure. Give garden plants a big drink (3 cups) of garden tea every two weeks all summer long. Also offer plants in pots a cup of garden tea every week.

Pages 122–123 show how to make compost and garden tea. If you like, you can use fish emulsion instead of garden tea. Buy liquid fish emulsion at a garden center and use it according to the instructions on the package.

Weeding

Whenever you see a weed, pick it. For big weeds, use a small shovel (called a trowel) or an old tablespoon to dig around the roots before you pull. If you find a weed near a good plant, hold the plant in the ground with one hand while you pull the weed out with the other.

Tip When plants are young, it's hard to tell weeds and seedlings apart. Wait until your seedlings are a few inches tall so that you can tell which is which. Ask someone to show you which are the weeds until you can tell for yourself.

Rake up tiny weeds with a cultivator. Drag the cultivator lightly through the dirt. (Stay a few inches away from your plants.) The cultivator will tear up small weeds.

 Even containers get weeds!

Mulching

Mulch is a thick blanket of stuff you put around your plants. It holds water in the soil and makes it hard for weeds to grow. Mulch can be compost, manure, straw, bark, grass clippings, leaves, sawdust, newspapers—even pieces of carpet!

Tip You can mix and match mulches. Put down a layer of compost first, then add some leaves or grass clippings later.

It's easy to mulch:

1. Wait until the plants are about 4 inches tall.

2. Spread 1 inch of mulch around the foot of each plant. As the plant grows, add more mulch.

Safety Note

If you use grass clippings, be sure the lawn they came from was not treated with weed killers. For containers, use any of the garden mulches, or use spahgnum moss.

Tip Some plants, such as strawberries, tomatoes, and cucumbers, grow low to the ground. Mulching with dry stuff, like grass clippings, keeps the fruit and veggies clean and dry.

Dealing with Pests

Aphids—Tiny, flat, pale-green insects that stick to the bottom of leaves. Look carefully—they are hard to see.

>**Prevention:** No way.

>**To Get Rid of Them:** Spray the underside of leaves with soapy water, or give them a hard blast from the hose (if your plants are strong enough).

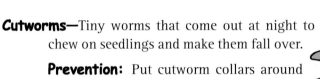

Cutworms—Tiny worms that come out at night to chew on seedlings and make them fall over.

>**Prevention:** Put cutworm collars around all your seedlings. Make the collars out of paper cups, cardboard tubes from toilet paper or paper towels, or even milk cartons.

Cabbage Worms—Cauliflower and broccoli are home to these little worms, which hatch from eggs laid by flies.

>**Prevention:** Put a worm mat around your seedlings so that the flies won't lay their eggs near your plants. Make the mat out of heavy cardboard or old carpeting.

>**To Get Rid of Them:** Pick them off the plants if you can.

Making a Worm Mat

To make a worm mat, cut a mat larger than 5 inches square. Then, cut a slit up the middle of the mat to the center. At the center, cut a hole large enough to fit around your plant. Gently slide your new worm mat around the plant and tape the slit shut.

Squash Borers—These worms live inside your cucumber and squash vines.

> **Prevention:** Make worm mats out of heavy aluminum foil.

> **To Get Rid of Them:** If some of the leaves on your squash plants wilt, a borer probably got into part of your vine. You don't need to get rid of the plant—just the stem that has wilted leaves. Cut the stem off at the ground and cover the stump with foil to keep other bugs out.

Mexican Bean Beetles—They look like tiny yellow porcupines. Look for them on bean plants.

> **Prevention:** No way.

> **To Get Rid of Them:** Pick them off, or pick off the holey leaves. If the leaves are lacy, dig up the whole plant and throw it away.

Tomato Hornworms—They start out small, eat like crazy, and grow into big, fat, ugly monsters.

> **Prevention:** Some people plant zinnias or marigolds near tomatoes to keep worms away. However, this does not always work.

> **To Get Rid of Them:** Pick them off with your fingers and throw them away.

Bugs That Feast on Leaves—If the leaves on your plants look holey, bugs are probably eating them.

To Get Rid of Them: You can wash them off with a blast of water from the hose (if your plants are strong enough to stand up to the blast). Spray the bugs with soapy water. (Dissolve $1/3$ cup Ivory™ soap flakes in 3 gallons of water.)

Pick the bugs off the leaves with your fingers or tongs. Pick off a whole leaf if it is covered with bugs, and throw it away.

If the plants are really suffering, with lots of leaves eaten to lace, dig up the plant and throw it away.

Don't worry that you've done something wrong: Bugs get the best of every gardener, sooner or later. Be sure to harvest whatever you can off the plant before you throw it away!

Compost 1-2-3

Compost turns your soil into a healthy home for plants. It adds nutrients that make your plants strong, and it makes the soil loose so that your plants can sink their roots into it. Making compost is easy—all you do is make a big pile. The pile does the rest.

Put In ...

Soil

Plant material:

- Old plants from the garden
- Grass clippings from lawns where no weed killers have been used for one year
- Leaves
- Fruit and vegetable scraps
- Manure from farm animals. You can get aged manure from a farm or stable, or you can buy it in bags. Bagged manure looks and feels like dirt, and it is sterilized to kill germs.

Keep Out ...

Meat or leftovers that contain meat

Eggs or eggshells

Diseased plants

Weeds

Twigs and pine needles

Compost in Three Steps

1. Find a spot:
   - in or near the garden
   - about 6 feet square
   - where you can leave the compost alone for several weeks or months

2. Make the pile.
   - Pile up some plant stuff. Rake the pile so that it is level.
   - Whenever you get more plant stuff, add it to the pile and rake it level. Do this until the pile is 12 inches tall.
   - Add 2 inches of manure. Add 1 inch of soil. Start over with the plant stuff.

3. Water the pile every week—unless it has rained.
   - Keep the pile damp but not soggy.

Tip You can get old manure from a farm or stable, or you can buy it in bags. Bagged manure looks and feels like dirt, and it is sterilized to kill germs.

Speed It Up

Your compost will grow faster if you mess it up every few weeks. Use a shovel or big stick to stir things up. Try to bring the stuff on the bottom to the top of the pile.

Keep Building

Keep adding layers to the same compost heap, or start a new one when the first one is about three plant-manure-soil layers tall.

Using Compost

You can tell when your compost is ready to use, because all the plant stuff will have turned into dirt. The whole pile will be dark and fluffy and crumbly, like a huge chocolate cupcake.

Compost pile (left), and raked flat (right). Here are the recommended contents for your compost pile from the bottom up: 12 inches of plant stuff, 2 inches of manure, 1 inch of soil.

Garden Tea

Garden tea makes plants grow strong! Give them a nice drink of garden tea once every two weeks.

1. Drop one shovel of old manure in a 5-gallon bucket.
2. Fill the bucket with water and let it stand in the shade for a few hours, until the manure dissolves.
3. Use an old cup to dip out the tea and pour it on the ground around your plants.

Tips for Growing Tomatoes by the Ton

Every gardener will tell you secret tricks for growing a bumper crop of tomatoes. But the biggest secret of all is: Tomatoes are easy to grow. After one summer, you will have secret tricks of your own!

May I Suggest

Early Girl, Better Boy VFN, and Roma VF are good full-size tomatoes.

Red Cherry and Super Sweet 100 are good cherry tomato plants for the garden.

Pixie, MicroTom, Tiny Tim, and Tom Thumb are good for pots.

Getting Started

- Tomatoes love rich soil. When you prepare your garden in the spring, work in lots of manure and compost.
- Tomatoes like heat and sun, so plant them where they will get lots of sun.
- Plant seedlings 3 feet apart if you are going to let them sprawl on the ground, or 2 feet apart if they are bush plants or you are going to grow them in cages (see page 23 or stakes page 101).
- Give your seedlings a good drink of garden tea (see page 123) to get them off to a healthy start.

Caring for Your Tomatoes

- Water your tomatoes every week, unless you have lots of rain.

- Spread a 1-inch-thick layer of manure around the plants two or three weeks after you plant them. Or give your plants a drink of garden tea (see page 123) every few weeks all summer long.

- Mulch your plants to keep their roots cool and to keep the tomatoes off the ground.

- Look for big, green, ugly tomato worms. Pick them off with your fingers and kill them.

Harvesting Your Tomatoes

- You can twist the tomato gently to break the stem. Or use scissors to cut the stem just above the tomato's cap.

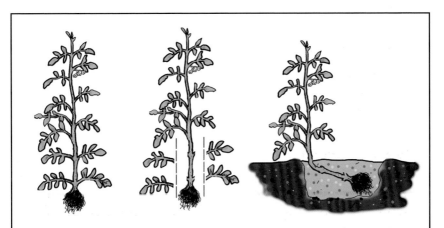

If your seedlings are more than 6 inches tall, take off a few of the lower leaves. Set the seedling in the hole so that some of the stem is underground. The leaf nodes that are underground will make new roots.

Glossary

bed—an area where the soil is ready for planting. See page 109.

bugs—see pages 118 to 121 for a glossary of bugs.

bulb—a plant's "storage area," like a seed in that the plant grows from it.

cage—a small fence that goes around tall plants to help them stand up straight. See page 23.

chop—cut into small pieces.

clove (of garlic)—one piece, or 'bud' you can break off a head of garlic.

compost—fertilizer made from plants, some kinds of food scraps, dirt and manure. See page 122–123.

compost pile—layers of dead plants, some kinds of food scraps, dirt, and manure, turning into compost.

curdle—to form little lumps in what you are cooking.

cutworm collar—see page 118.

dice-to chop into very small pieces

feed—fertilize.

fort—a small wall of dirt encircling a plant about a foot away from the stem, to hold water near the base of the plant.

garden tea—manure dissolved in water, a good fertilizer.

harden off—help plants get used to the outdoors by taking them outside for a few hours each day. See page 109.

hardy—plants that live in cold weather.

hill—a kind of raised bed, made by making a mound of dirt and flattening the top of it.

manure—animal droppings.

moat—a small ditch encircling a plant about a foot away from the stem, to hold water.

mound—a pile of dirt that is flat on top, for planting.

mulch—a thick layer of stuff—like bark, manure, grass clippings, compost, hay or even carpet scraps—spread out on the soil around your plants.

paring knife—a small, sharp knife with a short blade.

pruning shears—a garden tool that looks like big scissors. For adult use only.

rows—several plants planted one next to the other. Rows can be straight or squiggly.

Safe to Plant date—the date that is, *on the average,* safe to plant most plants. Every year is a little different; this is just a guide. See page 6.

seedlings—small plants, usually sold in four-packs or six-packs.

soil—dirt.

spacing—how far apart to plant seeds or seedlings.

sprig—a short stem with leaves on it. When recipes call for a sprig of an herb, just break off any leafy stem, about 3 inches long.

stake—a tall and thin but sturdy piece of wood, like a dowel, used to help tall plants stand up straight. See page 101.

stir-fry—to cook in hot oil, stirring constantly. This is a job for an adult.

tender—plants that are hurt by cold weather.

thinning—picking plants that crowd each other.

weed—any plant that is growing where it shouldn't.

wilt—go limp.

worm mat—see page 119.

Books for Gardeners & Cooks

Gardening

These books have lots of great ideas and information about gardens, from tea-cups on the windowsill to urban farms.

Bartholomew, Mel. *Square Foot Gardening.* Emmaus, Pa.: Rodale Press, 1981.

Crandall, Chuck, and Barbara Crandall. *Movable Harvests: The Simplicity and Bounty of Container Gardens.* Shelburne, Vt.: Chapters Publishing, 1995.

Creasy, Rosalind. *Cooking from the Garden: Creative Gardening and Contemporary Cuisine.* San Francisco, Calif.: Sierra Club Books, 1988.

Gilbertie, Sal. *Kitchen Herbs: The Art and Enjoyment of Growing Herbs and Cooking with Them.* New York: Bantam Books, 1988.

Hart, Avery, and Paul Mantell. *Kids Garden!* Charlotte, Vt.: Williamson Publishing Co., 1996.

Waters, Marjorie. *The Victory Garden Kids' Book.* Boston: Houghton Mifflin, 1988.

Cooking

Most of the recipes in this book evolved during my years of cooking for children. Other recipes were adapted or pieced together from existing recipes. They were modified to please young palates, to simplify steps, or to take advantage of fresh vegetables from the garden. The following books are good sources of recipes and general cooking instructions.

Betty Crocker's Cookbook. New York: Golden Press, 1969.

Brody, Jane. *Jane Brody's Good Food Book: Living the High-Carbohydrate Way.* New York: Bantam Books, 1987.

The Fannie Farmer Cookbook. Boston: Little, Brown, 1965.

Lee, Karen. *Chinese Cooking for the American Kitchen.* New York: Atheneum, 1976.

Creasy, Rosalind. *Cooking from the Garden: Creative Gardening and Contemporary Cuisine.* San Francisco, Calif.: Sierra Club Books, 1988.

Fun with Fruits & Vegetables Kids Cookbook. Dole Food Company, 1992.

Gilbertie, Sal. *Kitchen Herbs: The Art and Enjoyment of Growing Herbs and Cooking with Them.* New York: Bantam Books, 1988.

Hart, Avery, and Paul Mantell. *Kids Garden!* Charlotte, Vt.: Williamson Publishing Col, 1996.

Morash, Marian. *Victory Garden Cookbook.* New York: Alfred A. Knopf, 1982.

Norris, Dorry Baird. *Sage Cottage Herb Garden Cookbook.* Old Saybrook, Conn.: Globe Pequot Press, 1991.

Rombauer, Irma S., Marion Rombauer Becker, and Ethan Becker. *Joy of Cooking.* New York: Scribner, 1997.

Stone, Sally, and Martin Stone. *Desserts with a Difference: Delicious and Surprising Vegetable Desserts.* New York: Charles Potter, 1993.

Ziedrich, Linda. *The Joy of Pickling: 200 Flavor-Packed Recipes for All Kinds of Produce from Garden or Market.* Boston: Harvard Common Press, 1998.

Index